LIFE

WITH A

PURPOSE

LIVING
WITH A
PURPOSE

Nigel Scotland

SCRIPTURE UNION
130 CITY ROAD LONDON EC1V 2NJ

This book is dedicated to my wife, Liz, who 'lives with a purpose'. Special thanks are due to Nicole Fishenden, Rebecca Halifax, Lyn Goodwin and Christine Preston for word-processing and helping to improve parts of the text. I am also indebted to Alison Barr, editor of adult books at Scripture Union, for her guidance, encouragement and careful editing.

CONTENTS

PREFACE

Bernard Levin once wrote that he hoped to discover why he was born before he died! This surely is the one crucial matter which most people want to solve. It is an issue to which the Christian faith has a clear affirmative answer. We are here in this world to develop a relationship with Jesus Christ and to try to ensure that his presence and his teaching influence every aspect of our living. This includes our attitudes, our dealings with others, our work, our marriage, our social life, our politics and our service in the church. *Living with a purpose* is a clear, easy-to-read guide which gives a Christian perspective on these key aspects of everyday life that affects us all.

Although most people will read this book in a straightforward way, I very much hope that it will be useful in other contexts. *Living with a purpose* is based on the text of Peter's first letter, and the relevant passages have been inserted in the appropriate places in each chapter. This will be of particular interest to those who might want to examine more closely the biblical basis for some of the views expressed. In addition, questions have been added at the end of each chapter. Part of the thinking here is that church house-groups or other small study groups might like to make use of the material. A chapter of the book could be read individually beforehand or out loud at the meeting, then be followed by discussion of some of the issues raised. However the book is used, my hope is that it will serve to make clear that Christians of all people are those who can and should be *living with a purpose*.

NS

Chapter 1

A PURPOSE IN OUR EXISTENCE

In his novel *Hard Times* Charles Dickens gives a depressing description of the meaningless lives of the inhabitants.

> It was a town of red brick, or of brick that would have been red if the smoke and ashes had allowed it; but as matters stood it was a town of unnatural red and black like the painted face of a savage. . . . It contained several large streets all very like one another . . . inhabited by people equally like one another, who all went in and out at the same hours, with the same sound upon the same pavements, to do the same work, and to whom every day was the same as yesterday and tomorrow, and every year the counterpart of the last and the next.

This paragraph somehow captures so well the pointlessness and the futility of life for so many people. As I think about it, it takes me back to my days at Cockfosters in North London. Riding on the early morning Piccadilly Underground I often used to look at the lines of newspapers gently bobbing up and down with the motion of the train and wonder if this was all there was to life: forty-five years of going backwards and forwards through the tunnel to the City and a routine job; then, perhaps a decade of doing the garden and pottering around the shops; and finally, a few years on your own with continuous TV in some old people's home until the appointed day comes and the undertakers arrive. Somehow it all seemed so futile.

It is a fact that thousands do seem to cope with what John Keble termed 'the trivial round, the common task' and feel no need for anything further from their existence. Others, however, do get quite desperate that there seems to be no rhyme or reason for their being. In this feeling they are at one with the French existentialist novelist, Albert Camus (1913–60). In his novel, *Caligula*, he wrote: 'What is intolerable is to see one's life drained of meaning, to be told there is no reason for living.' Certainly Camus' words have been echoed by numerous others.

> Life is like an onion. You peel off layer after layer and then you find there is nothing in it.
>
> *James Gibbons Hunneker*

> Life may be defined as a rimless zero, a useless passion and an empty bubble floating on the sea of nothingness.
>
> *Jean-Paul Satre*

> We're all going to die anyway, so what does it matter so long as you keep a sense of humour and have fun.
>
> *Helena Bonham-Carter*

For most people, when we stop and think about it deeply, there has to be a reason why, some purpose to our being here, some point to our existence. The philosopher, Friedrich Nietzsche (1844–1900), made the point well when he wrote: 'If a man has a why for his life, he can bear almost any how.

The people to whom Peter originally penned his first letter (c. AD 60) were Jews from various Roman provinces mostly situated in what we know today as Turkey. Some of them had quite possibly become Christians when they were in Jerusalem for the Jewish festival of Pentecost. During the celebrations Peter had preached a sermon in the open air to some of the crowds thronging the streets. Many had accepted his message and entrusted their lives to Jesus. As a result they experienced God's presence in their lives in a new way as the Holy Spirit came upon them (Acts 2).

> Peter, an apostle of Jesus Christ, To God's elect, strangers in the world, scattered throughout Pontus, Galatia, Cappadocia, Asia and Bithynia, who have been chosen according to the foreknowledge of God the Father, through the sanctifying work of the Spirit, for obedience to Jesus Christ and sprinkling by his blood: Grace and peace be yours in abundance.
>
> *1 Peter 1:1,2*

These Christians lived in the Roman Empire at a time of persecution. In some cities and provinces this amounted to physical abuse of the most severe kind. Nero, the Roman Emperor at the time (AD 54–68), was a wicked and depraved individual, almost certainly mad. He demanded that his subjects call him 'God', and the political power in his hands clearly went to his head. He had an ambitious dream to build a new Rome but there seemed no good reason for dismantling the old city.

In AD 64 a huge fire swept through and destroyed large sections of the imperial capital. Contemporary sources reported that Nero watched the spectacular blaze from the balcony of his palace, rubbing his hands in glee that he would now be able to achieve his great ambition. In a very short time the populace got wind that Nero had instigated the fire himself and he became the object of bitterness and hatred. In order to divert attention away from himself he had to find a scapegoat and the Christians seemed an obvious choice. After all, he reasoned, hadn't their founder died a criminal's death and did they not teach that the earth would one day be destroyed by fire? Now here they were proving the point for all to see!

Nero began his campaign against the Christians by crucifying them in large numbers. Later he did far worse things. He dressed Christians in animal skins and set his hunting dogs on them. He even had some of them rolled in pitch and set them as human torches in the grounds of his imperial palace. So began a persecution of Christians which lasted, with varying degrees of intensity, for over two centuries. The Roman historian, Tacitus, wrote concerning the situation that Nero 'tortured some people hated for their evil practices – the group popularly known as "Christians".'

To many who heard Peter's letter as it was read out in the churches, life must have seemed quite futile. Numbers of them had been born as slaves with no rights and no status, enduring a harsh and gruelling daily grind with little reward, and much verbal abuse and brutal treatment. And now, to cap it all, because they had become Christians there was the prospect of further punishment, beatings and possibly a bloody end in some Roman arena. What point could there be to living under such circumstances?

Some of us may feel a sense of empathy with these early Christians. We may not literally be slaves, but we might be trapped by our circumstances at work or in the home. Equally, we may not be at the beck and call of an owner, but we could well be controlled by the manipulations of a colleague at work, a close associate or even a member of our family circle. Life may have turned sour: a broken marriage, a failed career, or someone we loved has died and left us feeling alone. Others of us may have suffered the pain and rejection of a redundancy or the failure to reach a goal we have set ourselves. A few of us have perhaps achieved all we set out to do and are now left with an empty hollowness because our needs still haven't been satisfied.

Whoever we are and whatever our circumstances, Peter begins his letter by emphatically stating that life *does* have a purpose: we are to live in this world as God's people. He is writing to fellow believers, 'God's elect', a term the recipients of the letter would readily have understood because, as Jews, they already saw themselves as God's chosen people. God has also 'chosen' us to be a part of his team, to serve and work for him in the world. When we become one of God's people, three things happen: we commit ourselves to Jesus, we experience Jesus' presence in our lives and we try to live our lives by his standards.

Commitment to Jesus

We live in a world where few people think of long-term commitment to anything, let alone people. Ours is an age of short-term contracts, temporary arrangements, casual relationships and trial marriages. Few people contemplate permanent commitments. Everything, including relationships, is expendable. Commitment to Jesus, however, has to be a once-for-all, lifelong commitment.

Why such stress on commitment to Jesus? The answer is because it is only Jesus who completely reveals God to us. Christians believe that somehow, in a way that we will never fully understand, the God of Israel was fully present in Jesus. This is something beyond our human capacity to rationalise. It's like trying to put all the world's oceans into a tea cup: it just can't be done. Yet this is the Christian revelation: that, in Jesus, God became a human being (John 10:30).

Professor William Barclay once related the story of a small boy standing in front of a portrait of his absent father. He suddenly exclaimed, 'I wish Daddy would step out of the picture.' This incident reflects in a limited way something of what happened at the birth of Jesus in Bethlehem. Down the centuries of Israel's history, people had gradually built up a picture of what God was like, which had come to them through their experiences, their laws and the teaching of their great leaders such as Moses and David. Later the prophets had clarified this picture still further. Then, at a particular point in time, the God of the Jewish nation 'stepped out of the picture' in the person of Jesus. Jesus, claims the writer of the letter to the Hebrews, is the 'exact representation' of God (Hebrews 1:3). Jesus himself said to his disciples that to have seen him was to have seen the Father (John 14:9). 'For in Christ all the fulness of the Deity lives in bodily form' (Colossians 2:9).

Although Jesus lived the life of an ordinary human being, there was one difference between himself and the rest of the human race: he was perfect. This is why he was and is able to forgive sins. 'Who can forgive sins but God alone?' was the astonished reaction of the religious leaders of his day, when Jesus pronounced people's sins forgiven (Mark 2:7). Martin Luther wrote about Jesus in this way:

> He ate, drank, slept, walked; was weary, sorrowful, rejoicing; he wept and he laughed; he knew hunger and thirst and sweat; he talked, he toiled, he prayed . . . so that there was no difference between him and other men, save only this, that he was God and had no sin.

Peter underlines that commitment to Jesus is vital by using the words 'sprinkling by his blood'. This idea comes from Exodus 24:6–8. When the people of Israel committed themselves to obey God, their leader Moses sprinkled them with blood – a way in which the ancients sealed agreements. Peter is making the point that, as Christians, our dedication to God must be equally as binding.

There's even more in these words because they also remind us that Jesus on his part made such a commitment to us that he shed his innocent blood for us. He died a criminal's death at a place of execution on the outskirts of Jerusalem, and it is through this death that God can forgive and free us from the sin and selfishness that grips hold of us so readily. It's a forgiveness which we have to make our own. In 1887 Queen Victoria marked the occasion of her Diamond Jubilee by issuing a free pardon to all those who had deserted from her armed forces. Details of this pardon were published in the newspapers. All that was required was that those who read the advertisements should write individually to the address listed and ask to receive a pardon. So it is where God is concerned. A free pardon is on offer. All that is required is that we claim it in person.

Experiencing the presence of Jesus

Becoming a Christian is more than committing our lives to Jesus, then relying on his word that he has forgiven us and will stay with us for the rest of our lives; it is also knowing the *reality* of the presence of Jesus in us. Peter refers to this as 'the sanctifying work of the Spirit'. The Spirit is the Holy Spirit who has been defined quite simply as 'Jesus' other self'. Just before Jesus finally left his disciples, he told them that it was better that he was going away because another Counsellor, the Holy Spirit, would be sent to them and would remain with them for ever (John 14:16).

The late Canon David Watson, a well-known evangelist, went on one occasion to a boys' boarding school to preach at their chapel service. When he got into the pulpit, he asked for a show of hands from all those who believed in God. There were quite a reasonable number. When he went on to ask how many believed in the Holy Spirit, not a single hand was raised. Then a small voice piped up from the front row, 'Please Sir, the boy who believes in the Holy Spirit is away this week!' This lad's comment is probably a fair reflection of the Christian church in many places! The Holy Spirit can so easily become the forgotten third person of the Trinity.

Some people speak as if the Holy Spirit were no more than psychic energy or an impersonal influence which operates in the world; but the Spirit is fully personal. Biblical evidence for this is overwhelming: Jesus says of the Spirit, 'When the Counsellor comes, whom I will send to you from the Father . . . he will testify about me' (John 15:26), and 'he will guide you into all truth' (John 16:12). The Holy Spirit is fully God, enabling us to experience the presence of Jesus in our lives and helping us to do the things that Jesus would want us to. Peter refers to this latter point when he speaks of the 'sanctifying work' of the Holy Spirit. The word 'sanctify' means to 'set apart'. Quite near where I live there is a large bird sanctuary, a land area set aside solely for migratory birds and other wild life. The Holy Spirit helps Christian people to set their lives apart for God. In very simple terms, to be 'sanctified' is to live our lives in a Christ-like way.

The Holy Spirit helps us to do many different things. He guides us; he speaks to us in the quiet of our own thoughts and consciences; he gives us the strength to keep going in demanding situations; he helps us in our praying and in our efforts to share the Christian message with others. These are all important things, but Peter brings our attention to the way the Holy Spirit can help us to live holy lives.

The secret of leading a good life, a holy life, is not that we should grit our teeth and strive and struggle to be like Jesus, although some effort on our part is important! The real secret is that Jesus, by his Spirit, can come and live in us and begin to reproduce in and through us the beauty of his own character.

Each person who makes the first initial step of becoming a Christian will have a conscious awareness of Jesus' very presence within them. Jesus promised to send the Holy Spirit to live *in* us (John 14:17; 15:26). Paul spoke of the 'mystery, which is Christ in you' (Colossians 1:27). What an amazing thing Jesus did by instilling his Holy Spirit actually in us. No wonder Paul spoke of it as a great mystery.

Jesus also spoke of the Holy Spirit as being like a spring of water flowing from the life of the Christian (John 7:38). The important thing obviously is that we don't do anything which might block or cut off that flow of God's Spirit in our lives. Just as mud and floating debris can hold back the water of a stream, so we need to keep our lives free from any activities or attitudes which block God's Spirit. This is why David prayed, 'Create in me a pure heart, O God . . . Do not . . . take your Holy Spirit from me' (Psalm 51:10,11). It's important that we should keep our lives as full of God's Spirit as possible. Jesus urged his disciples to pray constantly about the matter: 'How much more,' he said, 'will your Father in heaven give the Holy Spirit to those who ask him!' (Luke 11:13).

Obedience to Jesus

Being a Christian is more even than entrusting our lives to Jesus and knowing his presence in us. Jesus said that his true followers were those who not only heard what he said but actually did it in their everyday living. Those who took no notice of his teachings he likened to a foolish builder who built his house on a foundation of sand, which simply washed away when the storms came (Matthew 7:24–27). Jesus' life is a pattern for us to follow. Obedience to him means living our lives in the way that he did. It means shaping our characters by his teaching in the sermon on the mount (Matthew 5–7). When Peter speaks here of Christians having been 'chosen' for obedience to Jesus Christ, he means that we are to follow the example which Jesus set out for us. This is no easy thing. When we live in this way we will often appear to those around us like foreigners or exiles. We will appear, as Peter says, like 'strangers in the world'.

A year or two after my wife, Liz, and I were married, we moved to Canada where I was a parish minister for a time. We only had English passports with temporary visas which allowed us to work. We had no rights. We were allowed to stay only for a limited period. We couldn't vote in elections or have any say in the running of local affairs. The fact was we were 'strangers'. Although we loved the country and enjoyed the people, ultimately we did not belong there. Living as God's people means that we live our lives in this world to the full but, in the last analysis, we don't belong here. We are citizens of God's country and in the end we must live our lives according to the standards of the ten commandments and Jesus' expansion of them in his sermon on the mount.

This idea of Christians being exiles or 'strangers in the world' was beautifully expressed in an early Christian letter – known as the *Letter to Diognetus* – written at the beginning of the second century.

> Christians are not marked out from the rest of
> mankind by their country or their speech or
> their customs . . . they dwell in cities, both Greek
> and barbarian, each as his lot is cast, following
> the customs of the region in clothing and food
> and in the outward things of life generally; yet
> they manifest the wonderful and openly
> paradoxical character of their own (unseen)
> state. They inhabit the lands of their birth, but
> as temporary residents thereof; they take their
> share of all responsibilities as citizens, and
> endure all disabilities as aliens. Every foreign
> land is native to them and every native land,
> foreign territory . . . They pass their days on
> earth, but they hold citizenship in heaven.

Discussion questions

1 What purpose do you see in your existence?
2 What is your philosophy of life? How does it help you in times of tragedy or difficulty?

Chapter 2

A PURPOSE IN TRIALS AND PRESSURES

Peter wrote his letter against the background of terrible persecution and suffering of Christians which existed in the Roman Empire of the first century, and continued in varying degrees until the Emperor Constantine became a Christian in AD 312.

One of the most famous early Christian martyrdoms was that of Bishop Polycarp of Smyrna. When Polycarp was an old man, the Roman games were held in his home town. During the games excitement reached fever pitch and then blood began to flow. With the crowd shouting, 'Away with the atheists', eleven Christians were dragged to the arena and thrown to the lions. Eventually, the cry went up for the blood of Polycarp. Soldiers were dispatched to escort him from his little cottage on the outskirts of the city. When he came to the door, they failed to recognise him because he was so old. He could have escaped by saying that he had gone away; instead he allowed himself to be taken to the arena. When the governor saw how old he was, he told Polycarp that he only had to curse Christ and he would be free to go home. Polycarp refused saying, 'Eighty and six years have I served him and he has never done me wrong. How then can I blaspheme now my King whom I serve?' The governor was forced to allow his execution. By this time, the lions had been taken away so they burnt Polycarp to death in a huge fire. The wind blew the flames away from his body so that his death was agonisingly slow. People were so impressed by Polycarp's love and courage that they wrote a full account of his martyrdom.

In the twentieth century Christians in various places have suffered prolonged periods of intense pressure and physical hardship. In countries of the former Soviet Union to be a Christian was at best to be a second class citizen. It meant being regarded with contempt and to have one's children singled out for 'corrective instruction'. Many people all over the world are still suffering violence and physical abuse for their Christian faith. As I write, accounts are reaching the British press of the heartless brutality being meted out to the church in the Sudan, with reports of Christian people actually being crucified.

In England the Christian church is free of persecution, but this has not always been the case. In the latter part of the nineteenth century William and Catherine Booth established the Salvation Army at Whitechapel in the East End of London. The early Salvationists were pelted with rotten eggs and had their message shouted down by gangs of marauding youths. Catherine later wrote of their sufferings and took courage from the early Christians of Peter's day.

> It was an enthusiastic religion that swallowed them up, and made them willing to become wanderers and vagabonds on the face of the earth – for his sake to dwell in dens, to be torn asunder, and to be persecuted in every form.

We have to face the fact, of course that some trials are self-inflicted, for example workaholism which causes stress both to the workaholic and the people around him. Or a partner may leave because a spouse is so busy with other commitments that he or she stops communicating or making an effort to generate any kind of relationship. An instance which comes to my mind is that of a young lady who came to tell my wife and I how she had been sacked from her job as a sales person in a large department store because of her Christian commitment. Later, however, it transpired that she had been pestering customers and fellow staff alike with her particular brand of Christianity in a most insensitive and tactless manner. She had also apparently been 'preaching' when she should have been getting on with her work.

Having said this, the Lord often allows his people to go through trials *not* of their own making in order that they can fulfil his purposes. It may be an illness or some kind of physical hardship. Occasionally, other people, perhaps those with whom we live and work, may cause us frustrations, worry and sometimes bitter hurt. The Bible contains numerous examples of men and women whom God allowed to pass through trials and sufferings in order to accomplish his purposes: Job in the Old Testament, or Hannah unable to have the child she longed for. Then there is Jeremiah who was tortured and left for dead by the heartless citizens of Jerusalem who couldn't accept his preaching. And Paul who put up with his 'thorn in the flesh' for years while he did God's work. In more recent times we have witnessed the captivity of the Archbishop of Canterbury's special envoy, Terry Waite, as he tried to work for the release of political detainees. To all of us who suffer in any way 'in all kinds of trials' Peter expresses his conviction that God has a purpose in them.

Getting our priorities right

> Praise be to the God and Father of our Lord
> Jesus Christ! In his great mercy he has given us
> new birth into a living hope through the
> resurrection of Jesus Christ from the dead, and
> into an inheritance that can never perish, spoil
> or fade – kept in heaven for you, who through
> faith are shielded by God's power until the
> coming of the salvation that is ready to be
> revealed in the last time. In this you greatly
> rejoice, though now for a little while you may
> have had to suffer grief in all kinds of trials.
> These have come so that your faith – of greater
> worth than gold, which perishes even though
> refined by fire – may be proved genuine and
> may result in praise, glory and honour when
> Jesus Christ is revealed.
>
> *1 Peter 1:3–7*

Peter reminds us of the things that really matter, the hope that we now have as a result of our knowing the risen Jesus. He puts before us the great future inheritance 'that can never perish, spoil or fade'. We live in an age in which our energies are almost entirely sapped by the need to survive, grappling with the pressures of the rat race if we have a job or coping with unemployment if we don't. For those of us fortunate enough to have a regular income and a home of our own, there is the constant pull to increase 'all our creature comforts'. This kind of materialism has a very strong grip on many of us, probably more so as we grow older! It's the spirit of our era. It's so easy to become totally engulfed in the world of new cars, satellite TV, CD players, video recorders, the latest interest-free credit, furniture or kitchen suites, new clothes and exotic holidays.

There is, of course, a good side to ownership: we find a sense of identity and satisfaction through the things that we own. But we need to be on our guard because material things can so easily become all-engrossing. They can take our focus away from God and from the things that matter. They can make us greedy and unaware of the needs of others. They can also sap our spiritual power. In the Middle Ages a visitor to the papal treasury was very impressed by the vast piles of money. He remarked, 'I see that the church can no longer say "Silver and gold have I none".'

'True', replied the official, 'but neither can she say "In the name of Jesus walk"!'

Sometimes it's only when difficulty hits us or we suffer in some way that we begin to reassess our priorities. We see again the things that really matter. C S Lewis, in his book *The Problem of Pain*, spoke of suffering as 'God's megaphone in a deaf world'. By this he meant that we become so engrossed in other things that we simply don't hear God, until some pain or hurt brings us up with a start and we turn to God once more in consequence.

In the summer of 1990 I was in Addis Ababa, Ethiopia, with my wife and some other friends from our church in Gloucestershire, England. Ethiopia is a beautiful country with a rich history and long Christian tradition. However, ninety-five per cent of Addis is a dense jungle of shanty communities with a population approaching three million. A typical house in the city consists of a room of approximately ten feet square. It has walls made of sticks with old plants and plastic bags interwoven, a roof of rusty corrugated iron, and a floor of compacted mud that becomes a quagmire in the rainy season. There is no soap, no running water, no toilet and usually no electric light, no radio, no TV, no books, very little furniture, no clean clothes and probably one pair of shoes for each person living there. Outside the house are hundreds of narrow alley ways and passages. There are no street lights, no pavements and no police. Unless people are fortunate enough to live near one of the concrete pit toilets with new corrugated iron cubicles, they have to use open toilets – twelve foot square areas between the houses. For homes situated close to the toilet area, the stench and the risk of disease is devastating.

At the time of our visit, one of our group lived with her husband in a fairly small one-bedroom flat in Cheltenham. After seeing the suffering of Addis at first hand and the dignified way in which so many accepted it, she said, 'I will never complain about our flat again.' It not only changed her attitude in this matter, it affected all of us. We returned to the UK realising how much we have not only in personal possessions but in terms of food, health and housing. We saw how fortunate we are to live in a country which has peace and freedom of worship. Just seeing suffering can be enough to cause us to set our priorities to rights.

It was Dr Johnson who said, 'If a man knows he's going to die tomorrow, it clears his mind wonderfully.' One of the purposes in the trials and difficulties that come our way, can be to bring us back to things that are of real importance and of real worth. Peter reminds those who are suffering of the present 'living' hope that they have in Jesus Christ and of the final hope that they have in heaven. He underlines the nature of our salvation:

> Though you have not seen him, you love him; and even though you do not see him now, you believe in him and are filled with an inexpressible and glorious joy, for you are receiving the goal of your faith, the salvation of your souls.
>
> *1 Peter 1:8,9*

I've always enjoyed the story about Bishop Westcott of Durham who once was travelling in the same railway carriage compartment as a Salvation Army girl. Seeing he was a bishop, she had great doubts as to whether he could be a Christian! So she plucked up her courage and asked, 'Are you saved?' Bishop Westcott was reading his Greek New Testament at the time, so he replied, 'Do you mean *sotheis, sozomenos* or *sothesomenos*? – which put into English means: Do you mean "Have I been saved?", "Am I being saved?" or "Will I be saved?" ' Our salvation is, of course, all three of these. It began in the past when we first put our trust in Jesus Christ; it will be completed in the future when we meet with him face to face; but until that time, we 'are receiving . . . the salvation of [our] souls'. In the very simplest of terms, salvation is to be in relationship with Jesus Christ.

It's all too easy for us to become engrossed in secondary material concerns and to forget that the main point of our living is to grow in our relationship with Jesus. Paul put it like this: 'For to me,' he said, 'to live is Christ' (Philippians 1:21).

Is our faith genuine?

Some time ago I was helping one of our daughters to buy a second-hand car. I asked a local friend, who is a car salesman, if he would come with me to look at one particular vehicle which seemed promising. In a matter of moments, we were roaring down a nearby dual carriageway and then up a steep hill in third gear to see if there was any clutch slippage. Looking over his shoulder our friend commented, 'If anything's going to go, it will go now!' He was putting it through its paces to see if it was a genuinely sound car or not.

Not only do trials help us to keep our priorities right, Peter tells us that they come so that our faith 'may be proved genuine'. Someone once said, 'A man's devotion to any principle can be measured by his willingness to suffer for it'! When we stop to think about it, there is no other way than by trials that someone's faith can be tested. If we are Christians and we are passing through pain or stress, it could well be a sign to us that our faith is genuine.

In the Old Testament Job seemed to have a firm faith in God; but the taunt was made that he only believed in God because he and his family and his business flourished so richly. God allowed Job the awful test of losing first his prosperity, then his family and finally his physical health. Amazingly, in all this Job's faith responded confidently and remained steadfast. In fact, in the middle of it, Job called out, ' . . . [God] knows the way that I take; when he has tested me, I shall come forth as gold' (Job 23:10).

I was very challenged reading Dr Sheila Cassidy's book, *Audacity to Believe*. In December 1975 she was expelled from Chile by the government because she had treated a wounded revolutionary. Allende, the first democratically elected head of State, was ousted by the military junta in a coup on 11 September 1973. On 15 October of the same year there was a surprise raid on the outlawed revolutionary leftist party, the MIR, at their headquarters in Malloco. In the ensuing gun battle one man died and another suffered bullet wounds in the leg. On 21 October a Chilean Catholic priest asked Sheila to treat this man at a secret location. Acting solely out of compassion and without any political motivation, but obviously aware of the risks she was taking, she did so. Eventually the fact was discovered and Sheila was taken captive. She was stripped naked on three occasions, tortured with electric shock treatment and interrogated at the same time. Then she was interned for two years. Throughout this shocking outrage and brutal treatment Sheila's faith remained steadfast. She wrote at the conclusion of her book that the experience had taught her the truth of Jesus' promise to his disciples that 'everyone who has left houses or brothers or sisters or father or mother or children or lands, for my sake, will receive a hundredfold and inherit eternal life'.

In the crucible

God our Father may allow us to pass through trials because they refine us like gold being refined in the furnace. One commentator put it like this: 'As fire refines gold so, when the heat is on your life, dross will surface and twenty-four carat faith will gradually develop underneath'.

Someone was telling me recently of a Birmingham refinery which produces stainless steel. The refiners apparently know the liquid metal is ready for pouring when they can see their image clearly reflected in it. If the human image is obscured or blurred they simply go on increasing the heat until the requisite amount of impurities have been burnt off. In a similar way trials and difficulties can have the effect of refining out of us our hardness and insensitivity and generally removing our rough edges. Some of the world's most gentle and gracious Christian men and women are those who have experienced suffering of one kind or another.

The trials and suffering, which all Christians inevitably experience, either cause us to turn away from Jesus or draw us closer to him, if we submit ourselves in faith to his will. As Sir John Reith, the founder of the BBC, once said, 'I do not like crises but I do like the opportunities they bring.'

Training for endurance

In verses 8 and 9 Peter makes the point that, although Christians are suffering, their faith in Jesus is developing and growing stronger. They are being filled with 'an inexpressible and glorious joy'. It seems a paradox that, whilst experiencing trials and stresses, Christians are growing into a rich relationship with God, yet this is a fact of Christian experience which is widely attested. As I write this, the entertainer Roy Castle has just died. His obituary in the *The Times* (3 September 1994) reported that in his last years of suffering the pain of cancer 'his life was sustained by the profound Christian faith which he shared with his wife, Fiona'. Indeed, Fiona's faith has become stronger in this period of stress and uncertainty.

One of the reasons why we train for sporting activities is to increase our capacity to endure. If, like me, you are a regular swimmer and you struggle one week to complete thirty lengths, you will find that next week it won't be quite so strenuous. Hopefully you

will have added just that little bit of extra stamina
which will enable you to cope with a slightly greater
demand. The same principle applies where our
relationship with Jesus is concerned. If we have been
able to keep a good relationship with him even when
things have been hard and stressful, our capacity to
stick with him will have increased.

To illustrate this point we have only to think of all
the trials of Joseph in the Old Testament (Genesis
37–45). One can hardly imagine a more miserable
beginning for a young man's life. Nobody liked his
style, least of all in jackets! His brothers resented the
way their father doted on him, and they plotted to
get rid of him. The Ishmaelites, to whom they sold
Joseph, re-traded him at an Egyptian slave market
where he was bought by Potiphar, one of Pharaoh's
military staff. Soon he was in trouble again. He wisely
resisted the sexual advances of his boss's wife, and,
as a result, found himself in a foreign prison. But, in
all this, God was actually strengthening Joseph's faith
for a much greater responsibility which was going to
come his way as Prime Minister of Egypt.

Peter concludes his point by reminding the recipients of his letter of the great privileges of knowing
Jesus personally. This salvation was never fully understood by the great prophets of the Old Testament;
although they predicted the sufferings of Jesus that
made our salvation possible, they never had the privi-
lege of seeing it or experiencing it for themselves.

> Concerning this salvation, the prophets, who
> spoke of the grace that was to come to you,
> searched intently and with the greatest care,
> trying to find out the time and circumstances to
> which the Spirit of Christ in them was pointing

when he predicted the sufferings of Christ and
the glories that would follow. It was revealed to
them that they were not serving themselves but
you, when they spoke of the things that have
now been told you by those who have preached
the gospel to you by the Holy Spirit sent from
heaven. Even angels long to look into these
things.

1 Peter 1:10–12

One life which illustrates so well the positive benefits
of trials and difficulties is that of George Frederic
Handel. Towards the end of his life his health and his
fortunes had reached an all time low. His right side
was paralysed and he was bankrupt. His creditors
threatened to put him in prison. For a brief time he
was tempted to surrender to the pressure of it all.
Then he rebounded to compose the greatest of his
works, *Messiah*. The unequalled 'Hallelujah Chorus'
was born not in the music rooms of a monarch's palace
but out of suffering and harsh and restricted circumstances.

Discussion questions

1 Which pressures do you find hardest to deal with,
   and why?
2 Identify the pressures you experience which are of
   your own making.
3 Do you create pressure for yourself and those you
   live with by working more hours than the
   responsibilities of your work require?

Chapter 3

A PURPOSE IN OUR BEHAVIOUR

> Therefore, prepare your minds for action; be self-controlled; set your hope fully on the grace to be given you when Jesus Christ is revealed. As obedient children, do not conform to the evil desires you had when you lived in ignorance. But just as he who called you is holy, so be holy in all you do; for it is written: 'Be holy, because I am holy.'
>
> *1 Peter 1:13–16*

Peter gets down to the basics of everyday living. This has to do with the way we think and react to others and our own desires. Peter tells us here that, for the Christian, there is a purpose in every aspect of our behaviour. We are to 'be holy in *all* [we] do'.

I have been impressed by the ways in which some of the early British Celtic Christians showed this quality of holiness in their everyday living. In his *Confessions*, St Patrick related how he frequently prayed while he fed cattle or walked through the snow and frost on his travels. An important aspect of Celtic daily life was asking God to bless everyday domestic activities; no situation was too small to bring to him. There are, for example, early Celtic prayers for blessing the house and for taking a bath, for hatching eggs, for clipping sheep and for tending the loom.

We find this same emphasis on purposeful living in every aspect of daily life in the writing of the exemplary parish priest, George Herbert (1593–1633). In one of his well-known hymns he wrote:

Teach me my God and King,
In all things thee to see,
And what I do in any thing,
To do it as for thee.

The purpose of our every action is that we reflect God's character of holiness. I wonder what the word 'holiness' does for you? Possibly not a lot! 'Holy Moses', 'Holy cow', and 'Holy smoke' are heated American expletives used when things go wrong. 'Holy rollers' are religious fanatics who shout and scream and make emotional pleas for donations. 'Holy Joes' are a bit of an embarrassment to have around, with long faces, big religious books and a ready stock of verses to quote from the Bible. They certainly don't go dancing or to the theatre, the cinema, pubs or the football terraces. To many people 'holiness' is just another form of 'church-speak', like being 'saved', 'sanctified', 'washed', 'covered' and 'predestinated'. The meaning isn't clear but, as far as the average person is concerned, it denotes a benign 'goody goody', or the kind of person who goes to a lot of religious meetings in a week. The word 'holiness' doesn't have a very good press in the commercial world either. One of the main publishers of the Bible recently dropped 'Holy' from the title page of their Bible. A member of their staff commented, 'We dropped the word "Holy" to give it market appeal'!

Despite these misunderstandings and the bad image of the word, holiness is important. There are thirty places in the New Testament where Christians are explicitly told to be holy. This passage of Peter's first letter is one of them. We should therefore consider what this means.

Holiness in the New Testament means 'to be different'. In the Old Testament the Hebrew word means 'to cut' or to be separate. So the temple in Jerusalem was a 'holy' building: that is, it was separate from other buildings, a place where God's people met with him face to face. This was why the inner part of the building was called the Holy Place. Again, Sunday is often called a 'holy day' because it is different from other days, to be used for rest, relaxation and worship. The word 'holiday' is simply a secularised version of 'holyday'. Again the word 'holy' is used of God's Spirit because God's Spirit is different from all other spirits. One of the most frequent terms for God in the Old Testament is the 'Holy One'. It reminds us that God is above and separate from all other beings.

When Peter urges us to holiness, what he wants is that we be different in our standards of behaviour. One important point in passing, holiness means being primarily separate or different *for* rather than separate *from*. God wants us to live holy lives *alongside* other people, not away from them in religious ghettos. It's not sufficient to be in church on a Sunday. We must be active in the community on Monday. He wants us to be 'lights' in the world, not those who escape from it, leaving it in darkness. We are to be like 'obedient children', to live by God's standards, the basis of which are the ten commandments (Exodus 20). We must be obedient not just in our actions, but in how we think and feel on the inside ('minds', 1 Peter: 13) and also in our wills ('desires', v14). We won't be able to begin to achieve these standards by our own efforts. We need God's Spirit inside us to give us that added motivation and strength. If we have entrusted our lives to Jesus Christ and invited him to share all that we are and have, then he will give us whatever it takes to be obedient to him. In particular, he puts into us his Holy Spirit who will prompt us through our consciences and our thinking to holiness in our behaviour.

Even with the help of the Holy Spirit living in us, holy living is never going to be easy. The temptation for us is always going to be to conform to our own 'evil desires' (v14) and to the pull of those around us. Probably at no other time this century has so much pressure been on Christians to conform to the prevailing standards of society at large. In the area of family life, so many Christians are allowing their marriages to break up without sufficient effort to restore their relationships. In the area of domestic comfort, Christians are becoming taken over by the materialistic pressures of late twentieth century living. In the area of the work place, far too many have become 'driven', workaholic, performance-orientated zombies.

The call to holiness

Peter tells us that we are to be holy because God is holy. When we pray the Lord's Prayer we say 'hallowed' or 'holy be your name'. God is a loving Father but he is also holy, that is, he is totally pure and totally clean. The prophet Habbakuk declares, 'O Lord . . . Your eyes are too pure to look on evil; you cannot tolerate wrong' (Habbakuk 1:13). Time and time again in the Old Testament God says, 'Be holy because I am holy.'

When the Protestant reformer John Calvin studied at Paris University, his friends nicknamed him 'The Accusative Case'. The reason for this was not because he was good at Latin! It was because the quality of his life seemed to 'accuse' those with whom he came into contact of the things which were not right in their own lives. Most of us know one or two outstanding and godly Christians but, by and large, churches do not seem to take much notice of God's purpose that we should be holy in our everyday living. The number of Christians who, like Mary Whitehouse, stand out against the falling standards reflected in our national TV network are few and far between. The overall impact of vicars' misdemeanours and televangelists' scandals appears to leave the public with the view that Christians are much the same as the general run of society in their behaviour.

When Alexander the Great, ruler of the Greek Empire from 336–323 BC, was at the height of his power, his army was second to none for discipline and effectiveness. From time to time soldiers who had deserted from his forces were brought before him. On one occasion, a youth who had left the ranks was brought before him. Alexander glared down at him and yelled, 'What's your name?' The petrified youngster who could hardly stand up only managed to gulp: 'A-A-Alexander, S-s-sir!' The great general took hold of the lad by the shoulders and shook him violently and replied: 'Either you mend your ways or you had better change your name.'

The early Christians to whom Peter was writing knew the importance of upholding God's name by the quality of their daily living. Later Christian leaders began to write defences of the Christian faith to the Roman authorities who were persecuting them. One of the main points they made was the upright quality of their living. For example Aristides, in his *Apology*, wrote:

> The Christians, O King ... have received
> commandments which they have engraved upon
> their minds, commandments which they observe
> in the faith ... Wherefore they do not commit
> adultery or fornication, nor bear false witness ...
> nor covet what is not theirs. They honour father
> and mother and show kindness to their
> neighbours ... And their oppressors they
> appease and they make friends of them; they do
> good to their enemies ... If they see a stranger,
> they take him to their dwellings and rejoice over
> him as a real brother ... And if anyone is poor
> and needy, and they haven't food to spare, they
> fast two or three days in order to supply him
> with the needed food. The precepts of their
> Messiah they observe with great care.

The early Christians saw a major purpose of their living as being to reflect God's holy character to the world in which they lived.

Why should we be holy?

> Since you call on a Father who judges each
> man's work impartially, live your lives as
> strangers here in reverent fear. For you know
> that it was not with perishable things such as
> silver or gold that you were redeemed from the
> empty way of life handed down to you from
> your forefathers, but with the precious blood of
> Christ, a lamb without blemish or defect. He

was chosen before the creation of the world,
but was revealed in these last times for your
sake. Through him you believe in God, who
raised him from the dead and glorified him,
and so your faith and hope are in God.

1 Peter 1:17–21

The one thing above all others which should motivate
us to holy living is the high price Jesus paid to
rescue us from an 'empty way of life'. The first recipients of this letter were Christian Jews, and Peter tells
them that this way of life was handed down to them
by their forefathers. The Judaism which they had
known before they became Christians was a fairly dull
affair, which revolved around domestic rituals and
keeping prescribed laws. The word 'empty' implies a
lack of reality, even futility. Jesus has delivered us
from such an emptiness, but at what cost? Peter uses
a term with which we are not quite so familiar in the
twentieth century as people were in earlier days.
Jesus, he says, has redeemed us. The Jews were familiar with the concept of redemption.

One of the most remarkable stories in the Old Testament is Hosea. Hosea, the prophet, took for himself
an adulterous wife called Gomer. To start with, the
relationship seemed to be secure. But tragically, Gomer
returned to her former ways and left Hosea for another
man. So great was Hosea's love for Gomer that he
searched for her and found her. She had sunk to the
very depths of degradation. But Hosea ransomed her –
that is, he bought her back – for fifteen shekels of silver
and about six ounces of barley. Hosea's story is an
imperfect reflection of what Jesus has done. He has
purchased us away from our selfish futile ways, not
with money as in Hosea's case, but by pouring out his

own life blood on a criminal's cross.

Ernst Gordon tells the story of the building of part of the Burma railway in the Second World War by prisoners of war in his book *Through the Valley and the Kwai*. At the end of a day's gruelling labour the tools were counted. The Japanese guard insisted that a shovel was missing. He was adamant that someone had stolen it to sell to the Thais. When no culprit was forthcoming, the enraged guard pulled back the bolt on his rifle and yelled 'All die! All die!' At that moment an Argyll stepped forward and admitted to the crime. The Japanese soldier clubbed the man to death with his rifle on the spot. When the detail arrived back at their camp, the tools were counted again. No shovel was missing. The Argyll soldier had given his life to ransom his fellows from certain death. His courageous and selfless act led to a religious revival among the allied troops.

Our redemption was planned by God and, because of it, we have a motivation to live well now in the hope of a complete life in the future.

Let holiness show

Now that you have purified yourselves by obeying the truth so that you have sincere love for your brothers, love one another deeply, from the heart. For you have been born again, not of perishable seed, but of imperishable, through the living and enduring word of God. For,

'All men are like grass, and all their glory is like the flowers of the field; the grass withers and the flowers fall, but the word of the Lord stands forever.'

And this is the word that was preached to you.

Therefore, rid yourselves of all malice and all deceit, hypocrisy, envy, and slander of every kind. Like newborn babies, crave pure spiritual milk, so that by it you may grow up in your salvation, now that you have tasted that the Lord is good.

1 Peter 1:22–2:3

Peter concludes this part of his letter by reminding us of some of the ways in which this holiness should be seen in terms of our everyday living. In particular he reminds us that we are to have a 'sincere love' for our fellow Christians. Such love is not only to be seen in terms of outward acts of kindness and care, and words of affirmation, encouragement and support; it is to be *felt*. Peter urges us to 'love one another deeply, from the heart'. This was the good news that John Wesley brought to the arid, intellectual, lifeless church in eighteenth century England. He taught that God's love was not merely an outward action, although that is an important aspect of it. Rather, at root, love is the presence of God's Holy Spirit implanting the feeling of love in our hearts. 'God has poured out his love into our hearts by the Holy Spirit, whom he has given us' (Romans 5:5). The deepest part of a human being is the ego, that part of us which elates, grieves, hurts, feels anger; in short, that part of us which 'feels'. When our feelings are truly touched and stirred then we are more likely to take action. Certainly it was true of Wesley. Not only did he call himself God's steward of the poor, he worked to the end of his days on their behalf. In one of the last entries in his journal he recounts how he waded ankle-deep through the snow-covered streets of Bristol collecting money and clothes for the poor.

The story (probably apocryphal) is told of a Sunday school teacher who tried to remonstrate with a little boy who was disrupting her class. 'Johnny, do you want to go to heaven or not?' she asked.

'Not with this lot,' was his belligerent reply! Whether the story is true or not, it is a salutary reminder to us that, all too often, little love is lost between those who should be living as Christian brothers and sisters.

Do we love our fellow Christians? There is no escape from this test. 'If anyone says, "I love God", yet hates his brother, he is a liar' (1 John 4:20). More than this, true feelings of love will go on to issue in practical action. 'If anyone has material possessions and sees his brother in need but has no pity on him, how can the love of God be in him?' (1 John 3:17). Love for our fellow Christians in the developing nations means offering them opportunities and technology to become independent and self-reliant. It also means allowing them to do things for us and benefitting from their expertise and resources.

If we are Jesus' people, there is a vital point to our everyday conduct: we are to live lives that are 'holy' and be Christ-like in our standards of behaviour, in our attitudes, and in our love for our fellow Christians. This love must show itself in compassion and practical care.

Discussion questions

1 How can we make our behaviour more Christ-like?
2 What aspects of our living do we resent most? How can our faith in Christ help us to change our attitude?

Chapter 4

A PURPOSE IN THE CHURCH

The image that the church fixes most often in people's minds, be they practising Christians or simply passers-by in the streets, is one of crumbling irrelevance, of a windswept suburban corner dominated by a stark grey-looking building, St Derelictus with St Mungo-the-less. By the gate is a thermometer which announces that £80,000 is needed to deal with death-watch beetle in the roof, dry rot in the timber or bats in the belfry. The grass in the churchyard is very long, the paint has half flaked from the notice-board on which the only notice is a rain-soaked tatty piece of paper announcing a forthcoming jumble sale. The inside of the building is dark and damp, and the conglomeration of pews and other paraphernalia give it the appearance of a suburban bric-a-brac shop. The vicar, the Reverend Canon B C P De Ath, has served faithfully for thirty-seven years. He's looking forward to retiring in the near future!

A little girl was being shown around a large and rather gloomy parish church. After a while she said to her mother, 'Mummy, does God live here?' The mother was caught slightly off her guard and gave the matter a moment or two's thought. Then she said, 'Yes dear, he does.'

'Well if I were God,' the little girl replied, 'I'd move'!

Perhaps we may think of the church not so much as the building but, in rather more biblical terms, as the people of God. Yet the image we hold in the back of our mind is perhaps of a group of good, well-meaning individuals who are kind and nice. They come together on Sunday and sing endless choruses and enjoy a 'good word' from their leader. They attend their house group and prayer time but somehow neither they nor their fellowship seem to engage with the outside world. Many in today's world have found, like Malcolm Muggeridge, that the church has often obscured God and Jesus from view and made any kind of personal relationship with him difficult. Muggeridge wrote:

> One of the most effective defensive systems against God's incursions has hitherto been organised religion. The various churches have provided a refuge for fugitives from God – his voice is drowned in the chanting, his smell lost in the incense, his purpose obscured and confused in creeds, dogmas, dissertations and other priestly pronounciamentos . . . Plainsong held him at bay, as did revivalist eloquence, hearty hymns and intoned prayers. Confronted with that chanting, moaning, gurgling voice – 'Dearly beloved brethren, I pray and beseech you . . .' or with that earnest, open, Oxfam face, shining like the morning sun with all the glories flesh is heir to, God could be relied on to make off.

I'm glad God isn't as critical as Muggeridge!

I spoke recently to a girl who had returned to Cheltenham after a term away at university. I asked her how she was finding her church, which is a well-known one. She replied that she had not really got into it! 'It is,' she said, 'like belonging to a great big social club, with God as the excuse.'

With these kinds of images of the church in our minds, it's easy for us to lose sight of the fact that God has a real purpose for his people in the life of the church. As we look at what this is, we need to remember once again that the Christians Peter was writing to were Jewish whose ideas about the church were coloured by their Jewish background of the temple and the local synagogue. So Peter writes to them using images drawn from their Jewish religious experience.

Commitment to Jesus the head of the church

As you come to him, the living Stone – rejected by men but chosen by God and precious to him – you also, like living stones, are being built into a spiritual house to be a holy priesthood, offering spiritual sacrifices acceptable to God through Jesus Christ. For in Scripture it says:

'See, I lay a stone in Zion, a chosen and precious cornerstone, and the one who trusts in him will never be put to shame.'

Now to you who believe, this stone is precious. But to those who do not believe,

'The stone the builders rejected has become the capstone,'

and,

'A stone that causes men to stumble and a rock that makes them fall.'

47

They stumble because they disobey the message
– which is also what they were destined for.

1 Peter 2:4–8

If we are honest, we will recognise the fact that we
come to church for all sorts of reasons: to see our
friends, to fulfil our social obligations, to be seen to
be doing 'our bit' for the local community, to make
ourselves feel good, to do our duty, even to widen
our business contacts. It is surprising how when we
gather for worship on Sundays, our minds are often
wrapped up with other matters: PCC Agendas and
diocesan quotas, the latest directive from the elders,
or the decisions from the recent deacons' meetings.
Somehow the One in whose name we should have
come, the One whose church it is, gets pushed onto
the side-lines.

I well remember when I was a parish minister in
Canada encountering a lady in a neighbouring church.
After my sermon, she came and introduced herself as
a canon's daughter and a 'red-hot Anglican', but in
the next breath she went on to tell me that she found
it very difficult to believe in Jesus.

God's purpose in our involvement with church is
that we should be totally committed to Jesus. The
primary purpose of church is that our relationship with
him should be deepened and strengthened in every
way. Jesus, Peter tells us, is both the 'cornerstone' and
the 'capstone' of the church. In other words, the whole
of church life and worship from top to bottom should
be focused in him. The cornerstone is usually a large
stone at the base of a building. The walls of the building rest on it and are 'tied together' by it. Thus Jesus
is both the foundation of the church's life and the one
who binds together the different groups and indi-

viduals who make up the church's members. When two sides of an arch are built up they eventually reach a common meeting point at the apex. The capstone is placed at this point and has the function of holding the sides together and in place. Thus Jesus is the head over all our activities. As he writes, Peter has in mind a picture of the great temple in Jerusalem, built of solid but inanimate stone. Jesus by contrast is 'the living Stone'. He is alive for ever more (Revelation 1: 18) and so is ever present, with us 'at all times and in all places' as the Prayer Book so beautifully expresses it.

Commitment to relationship with other Christians

Commitment to the church also means being committed to God's people. Obviously we can't be personally committed to everyone within a church of a hundred or more members, but we can be committed to some of them. Someone has said that 'the measure of our commitment to Christ is how committed we are to Christ's people.' Indeed, if we don't love and care for our fellow Christians, how can we claim to love God (1 John 4:20, 21)?

It's important to keep reminding ourselves that the purpose of the church is not primarily about buildings but rather it is about commitment to people. If we come from a Roman Catholic, Orthodox, or Church of England background, we are often most handicapped by this misconception because many of our church buildings are full of brass candelabra, crosses, sanctuary lamps and ornate furniture. To some of us, to worship without a proper pulpit or to have Holy Communion without a silver chalice sounds like a heresy. As I was preparing this, I came across this line from Professor William Barclay. He wrote: 'One of the greatest failures in the modern church is that we have identified the church with what are "officially" known as church buildings.'

No Christian would want to say that church buildings are unnecessary, but they may be a hindrance. Peter stresses that the church is not bricks and mortar but 'living stones', men, women and children who have been made alive by coming into personal contact with Jesus, who is 'the living Stone' with a capital S, 'rejected by men but chosen by God and precious to him'. To be part of the real church is to have entered into a personal everyday relationship with Jesus Christ.

Often what are generously called churches are more like scattered piles of bricks. The people have come to the Lord but they are not joined together, except possibly for an hour on Sundays. Individual Christians need to be joined together in a spiritual building as we relate to one another in the Holy Spirit. Jesus' purpose is that his people be joined together. This doesn't mean that they have to be 'lorded over' by 'heavy shepherding' or house-group leaders. It does mean that we voluntarily commit ourselves to at least some people within the church's membership. We commit ourselves to care for them, to be concerned in their affairs, to pray with them, to help practically and materially if the occasion presents itself, to visit them when they are sick, to learn with them and to work with them in extending the Christian message to others. So, to be practical, to be committed to God's people means that if we have a difference of opinion or feel a sense of hurt, it is important that we don't drift away in self-pity or feelings of inadequacy. We sometimes use the word 'fellowship' to describe our relationship with other Christians. The word is actually quite a strong one and can be used to mean a binding contract. Our fellowship should carry us through minor disagreements and enable us to stay together.

My home town of Cheltenham has its share of 'spiritual gypsies' who never really settle down in one church or commit themselves to any group of people for any length of time. For some of them going to church is like going to a restaurant. They eat at one place for a few weeks, then try another with a slightly different 'menu'. One of the reasons why the first Christians were so effective was because they were people who were totally committed to one another.

Commitment to worship

It is often said that the first duty of the Christian church is to worship. Peter sees that the purpose of our being built into a spiritual house is that we may become a holy priesthood, offering spiritual sacrifices to God. Once again he has in mind the great Jewish temple in Jerusalem as a picture of how Christians should be worshipping. In the Jewish religion of Old Testament times, before the coming of Jesus, only the High Priest was allowed to draw near to God in the Holy Place in the temple. Now, Peter says, *all* Christians are priests in the sense that we have all come into the presence of God through our personal friendship with his Son. Priesthood in Christianity is no longer confined to a few specially chosen men as it was in Judaism. Quite the reverse, all Christians, be they men, women or children, are a 'holy priesthood'. God's purpose is that we should all of us draw near to him and worship him. The *Westminster Shorter Catechism* asks the question, 'What is man's chief end?'

The answer is, 'To love God and enjoy him forever.' It doesn't matter whether we're in our mid-week house group or in the church meeting on a Sunday, our most important function is to worship. Worship is the key to most things in church life. If we can get the worship right, everything else often falls into place.

Worship is a broad subject and in its wider sense, it covers the whole of our lives (Romans 12:1). However, in this context, Peter is clearly concerned with worship as it occurs in the context of the Christian meeting, that is worship as 'declaring his praises' (v9). The basic New Testament word for this is *proskuneo*. It is an intimate term that means 'to kneel down and kiss the hand of'. We shouldn't therefore be embarrassed to sing songs or use words in public worship that express our love and commitment to God. Many of the psalms, which were used in the temple worship in Jerusalem and in the synagogue services that Jesus would have attended, express this kind of love for an intimate personal relationship with God.

To engage with God and meet with him in an intimate way takes time. The same is, of course, true of any relationship. To interact fully even with a close friend or marriage partner doesn't just happen in a few quickly snatched moments. And yet, in some churches, a song or hymn is sung through with little thought for what the words mean. Surely the hope should be that the congregation will meet with the Lord in a direct and personal way. We need to come gradually, humbly and reverently into his presence. In this way people's hearts and minds can be fixed on God. I take this to be implied in Peter's exhortation that we should offer to God 'spiritual sacrifices' (v5). Only as we make a concerted effort to give ourselves to God will we experience his presence. A W Tozer said, 'Worship is to feel God in your heart.'

God's purpose for the church is that we be a worshipping people. Tastes and preferences vary a great deal when it comes to worship. Part of the reason for this is our differing social, cultural, intellectual and ethnic backgrounds. However, perhaps the church to which you belong needs to give more time and thought to the way in which it worships? Perhaps the worship lacks balance. Or does your church need to look at worship in a wider context? Is it helping church members to make a positive impact on the world outside or is it causing them to become introverted, withdrawn from the wider world? As Amanda Smith, a black American evangelist, used to say, 'It doesn't matter how high you jump or how loud you shout, all that matters is what you do when you come down!' The all-important thing is that in our worship we meet with God in a real way and offer our lives to him. As a result of this we live more effectively for him.

Commitment to scripture

Commitment to church means commitment to scripture. Central to all our church life should be the explanation of and teaching of scripture. Article six of the Thirty Nine Articles of Religion reminds us that 'Holy Scripture contains all things necessary to salvation'. Martin Luther defined the church as 'the gathering of God's faithful people where the pure word of God is preached'.

Christians believe that the Old and New Testaments are inspired by God and that, as we read them, he can speak directly and personally. It is clear that Peter regarded scripture as being of supreme importance because he quotes from the Old Testament (1 Peter

2:6–8), using it to show how it spoke to him directly about the coming of Jesus Christ and the effect he would have on people's lives.

At different points in time, the Christian church has overlooked the need for the Bible to be central in its life and worship. The medieval church became so taken up with its religious festivals and ceremonies, that the plain, straightforward teaching of the Bible was almost forgotten. The Reformation took place in sixteenth century Europe to bring the church back to the truth on which it is founded. Men such as Nicholas Ridley and Thomas Cranmer were burnt at the stake because they insisted in a dark and corrupt age that the church must be committed to the Bible.

Emil Brunner, the Swiss theologian, used to say, 'Let us read the Bible thinking constantly of our daily life and let us live our daily lives thinking constantly of the Bible.' As individuals and as churches we need to reflect constantly on all that we do in the light of the Bible. Our family life, our relationships, our work, our leisure, our spending, our discipline, our speech, our practical caring, all needs to be shaped according to the principles found in scripture. This is what John Wesley meant when he said, 'Let me be a man of one Book.'

1 Peter 2:2 talks about our craving for 'pure spiritual milk' which we need so that we can grow into maturity. The Bible is part of this nourishment and we should feed our minds and spirits with its truth. William Gladstone said, 'I have known ninety-five of the world's great men in my time, and of these, eighty-seven were followers of the Bible. The Bible is stamped with a speciality of origin, and an immeasurable distance separates it from all competitors.'

Commitment to witness

But you are a chosen people, a royal priesthood,
a holy nation, a people belonging to God, that
you may declare the praises of him who called
you out of darkness into his wonderful light.
Once you were not a people, but now you are
the people of God; once you had not received
mercy, but now you have received mercy.

Dear friends, I urge you, as aliens and
strangers in the world, to abstain from sinful
desires, which war against your soul. Live such
good lives among the pagans that, though they
accuse you of doing wrong, they may see your
good deeds and glorify God on the day he visits
us.

1 Peter 2:9–12

Peter reminds us that when people respond to Jesus,
two things happen. They gain a new identity: once
they were nobodies, now they are part of God's
people. And they see the issues of life with clarity:
once they were in darkness, now they see things in the
light or perspective which Jesus gives them. Churches
have a reputation for a variety of different things
including processions, flower festivals, jumble sales,
and Sunday schools, but our first call is *to declare* the
praises of Jesus, the one who has called us to himself.
We are to be a mobile and witnessing people. So how
are we going to witness to the community in which
we live? Peter suggests two ways: first, by our speech
(v9) and also by the quality of our lives (v12). 'Live
such good lives among the pagans that . . . they may
see your good deeds and glorify God . . .'

We mustn't feel condemned or guilt-ridden if days

go by when we don't speak directly about the Lord to someone. Our relationship with God is not dependent on the level of our spoken witness as is the case with organisations such as the Jehovah's Witnesses who have regular targets set for them. We must simply be prayerfully ready to use the right and appropriate moments as they come along. Nevertheless, perhaps the church of today needs to be working to a different theme song: not 'Oh when the saints go marching in', but 'Oh when the saints go marching out'!

Then there is the quality of our lives. We mustn't allow ourselves to become trapped by attitudes and standards which are out of line with the teaching of Jesus. Our lives must be 'unstained' so that the light of Jesus' presence in us can be seen to shine through us.

To sum up, what Peter is saying is that there is no such thing as lone Christians. It is God's purpose that we should be part of his church. We are to be joined together in a personal relationship with Jesus and with his people. And it is God's purpose that we should make up a spiritual 'house' in which God lives and through which his love and care can be expressed to the wider community.

Discussion questions

1 Can you be an effective Christian without being a member of a church?
2 The Church of England and other Christian denominations are regarded by many as dying institutions incapable of new life. How can they experience renewal?
3 What is most important, as far as you are concerned, in church worship?

Chapter 5

A PURPOSE IN SOCIETY

Some years ago I took an American friend to visit the town of Hereford in the west of England. During our time there we happened to pass the city burial ground. On the gate is the following inscription:

Revd John Venn MA
Vicar of this parish 1833–70
fell asleep May 12, 1890
Laid to rest in this burial ground
One of Hereford's Greatest benefactors
Founder of
'The Hereford Society for Aiding
The Industrious' 1841
Hereford City Museum 1856
A friend and a guide to the poor
His sister Emelia Venn was associated
with him in his good work
By love serve one another

Here were two people who had found their purpose in society. They had served to the full the whole community in which they lived. There are scores of others like the Venns whose work has been publicly acclaimed: John Wesley, 'God's Steward of the Poor'; Elizabeth Fry, the prison reformer; Lord Shaftesbury, perhaps the greatest social reformer among the intellectuals; William and Catherine Booth, founders of the Salvation Army; and, in our own century, Mother Teresa of Calcutta. And alongside these people, there are countless others who have found their purpose in society in unobtrusive ways.

A visitor to a small village heard that one of the locals was a true saint, a tower of spiritual strength and a giant in prayer. He decided to pay him a call. He found this man sitting in his shop. After a bit, the visitor asked him, 'What service do you do for the Lord here?'

'I mend shoes,' the old man answered.

'Yes of course,' replied the visitor, 'I realise *how* you earn your living, but what do you do for the Lord?'

'I mend shoes,' he was told and had to be happy with that. Here was someone who had found what he took to be God's role for him in society and he was content. That we all find our fulfilment in serving society in some specific way is clearly a major aspect of God's purpose for us.

The novelist George Orwell wrote somewhat cynically that 'We work because we have to and all work is done to provide us with leisure and the means of spending that leisure as enjoyably as possible'. Perhaps this is how you feel. There is always the danger that Christians may cease to find any purpose in the particular work they are engaged in. But Peter reminds even slaves (1 Peter 2:18–21) that there is purpose in their work. I don't take this to mean that we should be content with whatever job we happen to be in. If our work situation is hard to cope with and very unfulfilling then perhaps we should look elsewhere. What I think Peter implies is that we should do the best we can to find the presence and help of Jesus in our particular work situation while we are in it.

We are to respect the state

> Submit yourselves for the Lord's sake to every authority instituted among men: whether to the king, as the supreme authority, or to governors, who are sent by him to punish those who do wrong and to commend those who do right. For it is God's will that by doing good you should silence the ignorant talk of foolish men. Live as free men, but do not use your freedom as a cover-up for evil; live as servants of God. Show proper respect to everyone: Love the brotherhood of believers, fear God, honour the king.
>
> Slaves, submit yourselves to your masters with all respect, not only to those who are good and considerate, but also to those who are harsh. For it is commendable if a man bears up under the pain of unjust suffering because he is conscious of God. But how is it to your credit if you receive a beating for doing wrong and endure it? But if you suffer for doing good and you endure it, this is commendable before God. To this you were called, because Christ suffered for you, leaving you an example, that you should follow in his steps.
>
> *1 Peter 2:13–21*

Peter reminds us that it is the duty of Christians to be good citizens of the country in which they live. Against the background of the totalitarian dictatorial regime of the Roman Empire, he could hardly have suggested other than submission. Nevertheless, Jesus also taught a clear principle that we are to 'give to Caesar what is Caesar's, and to God what is God's' (Matthew 22:21). It is New Testament teaching that anarchy and rebellion are to be avoided. Paul, for example, expressed the belief that the Roman authorities of his own time had been established by God. To rebel against their authority is to rebel against what God had instituted (Romans 13:2). He urged Timothy to make sure that the Christians he was responsible for offered up prayers and intercessions 'for kings and all those in authority' (1 Timothy 2:1,2), so that people will be able to live 'peaceful and quiet lives in all godliness and holiness'.

Praying for those in authority

One aspect of this which is particularly relevant to people living in Britain is that we pray for and be supportive of our Royal family, prime minister and his cabinet colleagues. We all know that the British Royal family has been under immense media and public pressure in recent times. Everyone of us wants the crown to reflect high standards of behaviour, particularly in its family life, but it's all too easy to be critical and condemnatory. The Church of England is right in the emphasis which its morning and evening services give to prayers for the Queen and the members of her household. If ever anyone needed God's heavenly grace, our Royal family do at this moment. How much do we pray for them in a regular way in our private times of prayer or when we meet together with other Christians? Peter regards respect and prayer for the government of whatever country we live in as a vital part of our Christian commitment. The Caesars of Peter's time, godless and brutal though

they were, had at least brought peace and stability to
the middle-eastern world. This was why a Christian
leader like Tertullian of North Africa could write in
his *Apology:*

> Without ceasing, for all our emperors we
> offer prayer. We pray for life prolonged;
> for security to the empire; for protection
> for the imperial house; for brave armies,
> a faithful senate, a virtuous people, the
> world at rest – whatever, as man or Caesar,
> an Emperor would wish.

He goes on to say that the Christian cannot but give
the respect due to the position and authority of the
Emperor, because the Christian believes the Emperor
'is called by our Lord to his office'.

Being responsible citizens
We have a duty to our country. We may owe it many
things. We have a responsibility to our nation if it
provides for our safety against lawless men and gives
us other public services such as education, medical
services and protection against unemployment and
old age. But what about countries such as Rwanda,
Somalia or Chile where these services are not on offer?
Or what if a government abuses the rights of the
orphan and the widow and allows the poor to be
trampled on? This is an altogether different situation.
Please read on, I discuss this shortly! Nonetheless, to
fail to be a good citizen is to fail in our Christian duty,
though we are also citizens of heaven, 'aliens' and
'strangers'.

Our commitment must also mean that we try to
ensure that the country in which we live is as secure

and as stable as possible. Jesus calls us to have the qualities of salt and light: it should therefore be our aim to work for a society in which there is freedom of speech and worship, justice and equality of opportunity, the right to privacy, and true and lasting peace. Christians should be active in local government, in trade unions and in other areas of public debate. Have you ever considered the possibility of becoming a parent governor in a local school, or standing as a local council member?

Upholding the rule of law
This has two aspects. We are to support all those who have the responsibility of securing justice – our police force, for example; and we are to respect and honour the law to the best of our ability.

> Submit yourselves for the Lord's sake
> ... to governors, who are sent by him
> to punish those who do wrong and to
> commend those who do right. For it is
> God's will that by doing good you should
> silence the ignorant talk of foolish men.
>
> *1 Peter 2:14,15*

Once the laws of nations like Britain and the United States of America were all fashioned by and rooted in biblical tradition. But in recent decades the whole notion of punishing offenders has come to be regarded in many circles as a product of a bygone era. Adherence to the biblical principle of 'spare the rod; spoil the child' is no longer a very fashionable idea. Governmental negligence allows television and the media to influence young people in particular, and society in general, in the direction of crime, violence and sexual immorality and perversion. As Christians we need to campaign for a system of rational justice which recognises what is wrong and punishes offenders. And we need to do our utmost to keep the laws of the land ourselves. How good are we with the payment of our bills and or keeping to the speed limit for example?

Obeying God rather than men

Whilst our duty as Christians is to respect the state and uphold its laws, what if we live in a country where people's basic human rights are abused for reasons of race, colour or gender? Or what if the government of the country of which we are citizens forbids Christian worship?

Imagine for a moment that it's 1960. You are a black American parent. Your child is tugging on your arm wanting to know why she can't go into the public amusement park that is forever popping up on the TV adverts. What do you do when the state laws exclude you because you are black and therefore second class? For two centuries you have waited for equality and justice and still there's no sign of it on the horizon. Or imagine it's 1940 and you are a German Christian. You know that every day the Nazis are hunting out your Jewish neighbours and friends and herding them off in cattle trucks to concentration camps where only starvation and extermination awaits them. Can you 'submit to every authority' in such cases? Clearly not! Christians have a higher duty than respect for the State in which they live, and that is respect for God. There will be occasions, as Peter himself found out (Acts 5:29), when we must obey God rather than men.

Dietrich Bonhoeffer, a Christian minister during the

time of the Nazi rule in Germany, saw his church and his country in terrible danger and placed himself in the front line of the opposition. He said:

> When a madman is tearing through
> the streets in a car, I can as a pastor
> who happens to be on the scene, do more
> than merely console or bury those who
> have been run over. I must jump in
> front of the car and stop it.

In 1942, Bonhoeffer tried unsuccessfully to win the co-operation of the British War Cabinet in overthrowing Hitler. He was arrested and died in the concentration camp at Flossenberg on 9 April 1945.

Peter is simply asserting a *general* rule that we should respect and submit to the state. Our respect and submission has two provisos: it must be for the Lord's sake and it must be to a law which is in praise of good and which condemns evil. Clearly a government that passes laws which are *not* in praise of good cannot expect Christians to submit to it. We are, says Peter, 'to live as free men'. We remain in this freedom so long as we are careful not to use it as an excuse for unlawful rebellion against a government which is just in its essentials. There is something of a paradox here which Martin Luther expressed in his great treatise *Concerning Christian Liberty*. He wrote: 'A Christian man is the most free Lord of all, and subject to none; a Christian man is the most dutiful steward of all, and subject to everyone.'

Respect all people

> Show proper respect to everyone: Love the
> brotherhood of believers, fear God and honour
> the king.
>
> 1 Peter 2:17

Respect everyone

One of the problems of the highly computerised
society in the developed world is that people are
rapidly coming to be regarded as numbers. A person
may have a student number, a national health number,
a social security number. Somehow we in the West
have to learn to see past the next print-out and recognise men and women as persons in their own right.

In his novel, *Dangling Man*, the American author,
Saul Bellow, describes a man who is about to be drafted
to the war in Vietnam, and so leaves his job. Then, to
his astonishment, he finds that he is not required by the
American war machine after all. But his company have
hired someone else in his place and they won't give
him his job back. He feels alone, and that nobody quite
understands his particular situation. No one really
cares about him, and he's left just a 'dangling man'.

All around us there are 'dangling' people who have
lost their sense of self-worth and, in consequence, no
longer see themselves or their future in a positive light.
A man or woman who is made redundant feels a
sudden sense of obsolescence. A married person whose
partner suddenly deserts them is left bereaved and
hurt.

Peter tells us here that we are to respect people in
general. What does this mean in everyday practical
terms? Perhaps one simple way of putting it is to treat
people in the same way that Jesus treated them, to

follow his 'golden rule' of doing to others as we would have them do to us (Matthew 7:12). Jesus had time for people: he sat and listened to them; wherever possible he met them at their point of need. He felt for them and had compassion (sometimes translated 'a tender heart') for them. He spoke honestly to them, but graciously and kindly. Jesus showed his appreciation and affection. One of the major characteristics of treating people with respect is to be compassionate towards them. Jesus identified hardness of heart as the root cause of divorce (Matthew 19:7–9). There are too many hard-hearted people even in the Christian world today. We constantly read of Jesus that he was moved with compassion, that his heart went out to individuals like the rich young ruler (Matthew 19:16–22) or the twisting tax collector, Zacchaeus (Luke 19:1–10).

So how do we measure up to Peter's teaching about respect for others? Are we patient and kind? Are we warm-hearted and outgoing to those who cross our paths? Do we listen carefully and give the other person our undivided attention? If we are parents, do we respect our children by giving them time and doing things with them? If we are in business and carry many pressures, do we make a conscious effort to wind down before returning at the end of the day so that we don't carry those stresses and strains back home with us? If we are in Christian work, are we taking time to be with our partner and family? Or could it be that our 'work for the Lord' is causing us a lack of respect for those who are dearest and closest to us?

Treating people with respect involves a wide range of attitudes, words and actions. It's so easy to thank people who do things for us and yet our carelessness

can easily cause us to forget. Telling people they do
things well can be such an encouragement. Showing
our appreciation by a 'thank you' note or a small gift
or flowers can all be means of showing our respect
and honouring people for what they have done. We
must never use anyone simply for our own ends.
We have a responsibility to respect people and to
honour them as those for whom Christ died.

'Love the brotherhood'
Within the Christian fellowship, our relationships
should operate at a deeper and more committed level.
The atmosphere that pervades the church should
always be one in which love predominates (John
13:34,35). The church is spoken of by Paul as the whole
family of God (Romans 8:14–17). Just as a happy
family is marked by a deep reciprocal love on the part
of its members, so the church as God's family is to be
marked by the badge of caring Christian love. It was
said of the early believers 'see how these Christians
love one another'. It was the loyal love among the
members of the first Christian church in Jerusalem
(Acts 2:42–47) which attracted so many newcomers
into membership.

Some of the New Testament churches didn't
measure up to this standard! The one at Corinth, for
example, suffered from party strife and factions (1
Corinthians 1:11,12), and the church at Ephesus lost
its first intense love (Revelation 2:2–6). Most, it seems,
did keep to this rule of love. When they met, they
would greet one another with a kiss of love (1 Thessalonians 5:26). They had a weekly meal called an *agape*
or love feast. At the end of this supper, which they
shared together, they ate and drank bread and wine
to symbolise the greatest act of love that this world

has witnessed (1 Corinthians 11:23–26).

We need frequently to assess the level of our love for God's people. How do we speak of the church and its leaders when we are away from it? Are we positive in the comments we make or are we negative and disparaging? If things are not as they should be in our church or fellowship, are we willing to go and talk to the person or persons concerned rather than grumbling about the matter? We are urged to speak the truth in love (Ephesians 4:15). Do we take the trouble to correct people's misunderstandings? Are we prepared to make an effort towards those who misrepresent us or give us the cold shoulder? All of these things are the marks of people who operate their lives on the basis of love. Paul in his famous hymn about love in 1 Corinthians 13, tells us that 'love builds up'. Do we look for what is positive and build up the people in our church fellowship by complimenting them and thanking them when appropriate? Or do we speak negatively in a situation? The New Testament tells us to do all things without grumbling. The message of the cross, as Reinhardt Bonnke has so clearly stated in his book, is from *Minus to Plus*. Love is positive.

Respect the king

Of all the injunctions in this verse, this is perhaps the more surprising. The king at the time when Peter wrote these words was none other than the Emperor Nero, in all probability the most ruthless, brutal and bloody of all the Caesars who ever held sway over the Roman Empire, although Domitian was a close contender! The New Testament teaches that the ruler is sent by God to preserve order in a nation. So long as he or she fulfils that function without standing contrary to the ways of God, they are to be respected.

Respect your employer

We live in an age when many employers are finding
themselves under pressure, often of their management's designing. All about us is the insecurity created
by fixed-term contracts, and the tension and stress
which goes with performance-related pay. In addition,
there is the related dishonesty and unhealthy competi-
tive struggling between colleagues. The middle-class
work ethic is in many cases as bad in its consequences
as 'the whip and strap' of the factory overseer and
the interminable hours worked by labourers in the
industrial revolution. But because we are living in a
time of high unemployment there is a constant fear of
redundancy. People feel compelled therefore to accept
hours and workloads which in better economic times
they would have resisted as unreasonable. All of this
is reaping a heavy toll on people's health, their family
life and relationships. It's not difficult to see why
many these days are resentful and often bitter towards
their employers. One sometimes wonders whether the
financial cost of all of this isn't far greater in the long
term than the money which companies generate by
misuse of their workforces.

There are, of course, good employers who are caring
and sensitive and pay well. However, supposing a
Christian finds himself in the employ of a harsh and
unreasonable boss, how is he or she to react? Amazing
as it may seem, Peter says that in such a situation the
Christian is to show respect. He writes: 'Slaves, submit
yourself to your masters with all respect, not only to
those who are good and considerate, but also to those
who are harsh.'

Some people wonder why Peter and the other

apostles did not take a stand against slavery. After all it's clear enough that slavery is contrary to the will of God and the New Testament principle that in Christ there is neither male or female, slave or free. However, the entire society of the Roman Empire existed on slavery. Under the rule of the Caesars in the first century AD, there are estimated to have been sixty million slaves. Slaves employed in labour gangs lived under appalling conditions and were literally worked to death. The lot of domestic and professional slaves was usually much better; sometimes there was even a warm and positive relationship between master and slave. But all slaves had one thing in common: they were mere chattels with no rights. They could be tortured and put to death by their master for any or no offence. If the young Christian church had challenged this system head on, it would have been crushed as a subversive, revolutionary cult. At one level, therefore, in advising slaves to be submissive to their employers, Peter was giving the only advice that made any sense. However, it would be quite wrong to suggest on this basis that Christians should teach total submission in all circumstances to injustice and heartless brutality in their work places.

All this is not to say that these words of Peter have no practical relevance for us today. Clearly they have! The principle here is similar to that which Peter urged on free citizens in their relationship with the state authorities (1 Peter 2:13–16). We are to show respect for our employers by doing our best to carry out their wishes and working diligently. We are to work in this way because we are conscious that God sees the situation fully and ultimately we are working for him. It is not a burden or a chore, but is our service to the Lord himself.

'He committed no sin, and no deceit was found
in his mouth.'

When they hurled their insults at him, he did
not retaliate; when he suffered, he made no
threats. Instead, he entrusted himself to him who
judges justly. He himself bore our sins in his body
on the tree, so that we might die to sins and live
for righteousness; by his wounds you have
been healed. For you were like sheep going
astray, but now you have returned to the
Shepherd and Overseer of your souls.

1 Peter 2:22–25

Sometimes a situation may seem just too much to
bear, and if such is the case, Peter urges us to get help
and strength from Jesus, the perfect example of unjust
suffering. As he hung on the cross, he experienced the
pain and the hurt of cruel verbal abuse, but he refused
to retaliate. He bore the agony of unjust physical abuse
without any revengeful action. More than that, as
Jesus hung on the cross he somehow drew into his
flesh all the unjust hurt and pain which has impacted
itself on us. He absorbed it into his own body (1 Peter
2:24) in the same way that a boiling hot dressing
draws the pain and poison out of a septic and pus-
filled wound. So Jesus can bring us emotional and
physical healing in the situation of hurt, not only at
our place of work but anywhere. By his wounds you
have been healed!

Discussion questions
1 In what aspects should Christians and churches be
   seeking to make an impact on society?
2 As a Christian, what aspects of the British state do
   you find difficult to respect?

Chapter 6

A PURPOSE IN MARRIAGE

A lady once approached Winston Churchill at a social occasion and said, 'Winston, if I were married to you, I would put poison in your coffee.' He is reputed to have replied, 'Madam, if I were married to you, I'd drink it!' A delightful piece of innocent banter in an era when marriage was a reasonably secure institution. Today sadly, as we are witnessing, society is crumbling with marital breakdown on a wide scale. Indeed the UK government is now proposing a no-fault divorce package in which partners can end their relationship after one year.

For some, marriage still evidently has that indefinable something. Annabel Harman, a writer and former television presenter, happily anticipating husband number five, said, 'I absolutely love being married, I think it's so cosy.' Elizabeth Taylor has been married eight times, Cary Grant five, Frank Sinatra, Dudley Moore, Joan Collins and Jane Seymour four, and Andrew Lloyd Webber and Bruce Forsyth three. However, it isn't just the world at large where marriage is a collapsing institution. Even some of the church's prominent leaders have become part of what seems to be an ever growing trend. Statistics show that in this country 170,000 marriages are failing every year. In parts of California one marriage in every two is now leading to divorce.

I am conscious that for some who are reading this marriage may not have a very positive image. Perhaps you have suffered the hurt, pain and rejection of a divorce. Perhaps your relationship is stormy or uncommunicative or dead. Some of us may be married and be finding the going hard. Some of us may have been happily married and have lost our partner. Others of us would like to have been married; some are still hoping they will be. Some may be living together, believing that legal formalities don't really count for much these days. Yet others of us will be single and genuinely believe that this is what God has called us to. On this matter we should be very clear that the single state is a spiritual gift (1 Corinthians 7:7).

Whatever our individual situation, the joining together of one man and one woman in marriage should be of concern to all Christians because marriage is a uniquely Christian institution. At its best, the church is a family. Those who are single may be able to support those who are married by praying and giving emotional support and practical help where possible. Conversely, those who are married can also offer friendship and support to those who are on their own.

The Report of the Royal Commission on Marriage and Divorce published in 1955 defined marriage as 'A voluntary union for life of one man and one woman to the exclusion of all others, that is to be regarded as voluntary, permanent, and strictly monogamous'. Marriage, according to the recently produced *Church English Dictionary*, was invented by God 'to create an environment strong enough to contain laughter, despair, sex, routine anniversaries, children, honesty, crises, dishonesty and in-laws'. Peter states that God has an even higher purpose for marriage. It is that husband and wives will realise their full potential as 'heirs ... [together] of the gracious gift of life'.

In order to help us in the direction of achieving God's purpose in marriage, Peter gives advice to both wives and husbands. As we look at what he says we may be struck by the fact that he gives the wives six times more advice than the men! The reason for this may be quite simply that there were many more women than men in the early Christian churches. We know, for example, that the Philippian church when it began consisted solely of women, nineteen in all.

Wives

> Wives, in the same way be submissive to your husbands so that, if any of them do not believe the word, they may be won over without words by the behaviour of their wives, when they see the purity and reverence of your lives. Your beauty should not come from outward adornment, such as braided hair and the wearing of gold jewellery and fine clothes. Instead, it should be that of your inner self, the unfading beauty of a gentle and quiet spirit, which is of great worth in God's sight. For this is the way the holy women of the past who put their hope in God used to make themselves beautiful. They were submissive to their own husbands, like Sarah, who obeyed Abraham and called him her master. You are her daughters if you do what is right and do not give way to fear.
>
> *1 Peter 3:1–6*

Peter gives wives three guidelines. First of all, he urges them to be submissive to their husbands (1 Peter 3:1). The word that he actually uses here is a military word which means to be under someone else's command! The same word is found in other places in the New Testament. It is part of a general household code which the early Christian leaders appear to have taught in the churches for which they were responsible. As this point, we need care in interpreting what this actually means for us today. Peter isn't telling wives to be a Christian version of Charles Dickens' Mrs Bumble whose husband declared, 'It is man's prerogative to command and the woman's duty to obey.' In fact Peter isn't referring solely to Christian husbands. He is also addressing women who have husbands who are not Christians on how best to handle their situation.

In the first century AD women were treated very badly. They had no rights and no status. The morning service at the Jewish synagogue was a men-only affair at which each worshipper gave thanks that God had not made him a gentile, a slave or a woman! A first century Jewish husband could divorce his wife for adultery, but a first century Jewish wife could not divorce her husband for the same offence. In the pagan world beyond the synagogue, the lot of women was even worse. In such a world a husband who was not a Christian was not likely to be won over by a Christian wife who lectured him about the Christian ideal of partnerships or sexual equality. Rather, Peter urges the Christian wife to submit to her husband in the way that most first century wives, Christian or otherwise, would have done, so that 'they may be won over without words by the behaviour of their wives'. This does not mean the husband has the right to turn his wife into a 'living doll'. The Christian wife needs to resist any attempt to undermine her integrity.

A husband and wife who relate to each other on a give-and-take basis are far more likely to produce a close relationship of mutual respect and love for each other. The opposite approach – a master-slave relationship – will only produce resentment and bitterness. Part of the problem is that we have been conditioned by twentieth century attitudes into thinking that to be submissive is the mark of a weak person who lacks conviction and doesn't know their own mind. We need to look again at Jesus and to recognise that he saw submissiveness as a strength. This is not to imply that Jesus was anyone's puppet. His submission to God meant that he stood firm against the religious leaders of his day and those who traded in the temple (Matthew 21:12,13); it also meant that he was submissive to Pilate and to those who took his life.

The second piece of advice that Peter gives to wives is not to go over the top on make up, jewellery and clothes. 'Your beauty should not come from outward adornment, such as braided hair and the wearing of gold jewellery and fine clothes. Instead, it should be that of your inner self, the unfading beauty of a gentle and quiet spirit, which is of great worth in God's sight.'

Again, we need to be careful how we read these verses. Pale faces and dull, boring clothes don't necessarily get high marks on the Christian holiness scale! Our dress and appearance are important but, having said that, it's all too easy for all of us, men and women, to overspend on clothes and toiletries.

Ultimately what is really going to count (v4) is 'the unfading beauty of a gentle and quiet spirit, which is of great worth in God's sight'.

In verse 5 Peter gives the example of Sarah, the ultimate role model of the perfect submissive wife. You may notice that she called Abraham, 'My Master' or 'My Lord' (AV). Again, we're not intended to take this literally as, for example, the Rastafarians do. (The Rastafarians originated in the West Indies. They were inspired by the preaching of Marcus Garvey who taught that a black messiah would come out of Africa to release the oppressed black peoples of the world. Rastafarians believe that this messiah was the late Emperor of Ethiopia, Haile Selassie.) Rastafarians treat all the scriptures very literally, and a Rasta woman is therefore expected to call her husband 'My Lord', as Sarah called Abraham, and to devote her whole working day attending to his every wish!

The last piece of advice that Peter gives to Christian women is do what is right without being afraid. Be submissive to their husbands wherever possible, yes. Be attractive and lovely and more important, cultivate the unfading beauty of God's spirit, yes. But be resolved not to compromise on God's standards. If it comes down to their husbands wanting them to do something which is contrary to what Jesus would wish, Peter says wives must 'do what is right and not give way to fear'.

Husbands

> Husbands, in the same way be considerate as
> you live with your wives, and treat them with
> respect as the weaker partner and as heirs with
> you of the gracious gift of life, so that nothing
> will hinder your prayers.
>
> *1 Peter 3:7*

Peter's advice to husbands, given in the New International Version of the Bible as ' . . . be considerate as you live with your wives', can also be translated 'be in subjection to'. It is interesting because, whilst Peter was writing first to Christian wives whose husbands were not Christians, now he is clearly addressing Christian husbands who had Christian wives. The reason for this is that in a world where women were totally subservient, it would be expected that if a man became a Christian, his wife would automatically follow him. But here Peter is telling Christian husbands of the first century that, even though society regarded women as second class and subservient, they must nevertheless respect and submit to their wives if the occasion requires it. Jesus emphasised that men and women are equal in the sight of God. The same point is made in other places in the New Testament (eg Galatians 3:28).

So in a Christian marriage the picture that emerges is one in which husband and wife both submit to each other. In Ephesians 5 Paul prefaces his discussion on marriage with the general principle that all Christians should '*submit* to one another out of reverence for Christ' (Ephesians 5:21). And in a discussion about sex in marriage in 1 Corinthians 7:3, Paul says that if the wife wants to make love, the husband should submit to her and vice versa.

Mutual submission is an important principle in all Christian relationships and none more so than marriage. If we want to get on with people, we have to learn to give and take. The Chinese have a proverb: 'The tree which bends in the wind a little, stands the longest'. A lot of relationships, and marriages in particular, breakdown because neither party will bend.

A further piece of advice to the husbands is to treat their wives 'with respect as the weaker partner'. The 'weaker partner' I take simply to be a reference to the fact that generally speaking, women are physically not as strong as men. Obviously women are equal with men intellectually and in every other respect. However, it's all too easy for those of us who are husbands to take our wives for granted, to work long hours and return home late, be incommunicative and then expect our wives to fit in with our plans. Such behaviour hardly squares with Peter's injunction to husbands here in verse 7 to 'respect' their wives. This means making time to be together, to listen to each other, to find out how the other feels and to do things together.

So what does all this add up to? If we can pattern marriage according to Peter's principle, we can hopefully begin to reach towards God's overall purpose for marriage, that husband and wife become *fellow heirs* of the gracious gift of life (v7). In the Eastern Orthodox Church tradition this purpose is beautifully reflected in the wedding service: after the husband and wife have made their vows to each other, they sit on two thrones and crowns are placed on their heads to remind them that they are joint heirs of all God's gifts.

A number of studies of marriage have identified a growing incidence of the opposite phenomenon known as 'married singleness'. In this state, couples who are married often live entirely separate lives. They go their own separate ways, pursue different objectives and have little or no shared emotional energy, activity or communication. What Peter is underlining in this picture of the husband and wife as '*joint* heirs' is that Christian couples who live a life of 'married singleness' cannot even begin to realise the potential which God has for them. God's rich inheritance comes to married couples jointly because they are joint heirs. Clearly all marriages need to work at being a couple, not two isolated singles!

Part of any couple's ability to receive jointly all that God has for them lies in their ability to pray together. Peter concludes this section by stressing just how important it is that 'nothing . . . [should] hinder your prayers'. Some Christian couples may find praying together a difficult matter. If this is the case, then maybe the way forward is to talk to the minister of your church or, better still, find another Christian couple who do pray together and get some help from them. It has been said that 'praying together is the heart of a Christian marriage. It is the cement which binds the couple to each other and to Jesus'. Whilst we may find it difficult to do this, Peter's assumption seems to be that married couples will make praying together a regular part of their lives.

In conclusion, we must steer clear of that mind-set which sees a marriage from the perspective of one partner only. Neither party in a marriage is going to be either blessed or realise God's full potential for them unless they plan, share and work together in concert. God's purpose is for husband and wife to be joint heirs of his 'gracious gift of life'.

Discussion questions

1 How can we 'affair-proof' our marriages?
2 What factors, in your view, contribute to marital breakdown at the present time?
3 What did Peter mean when he wrote that wives were to 'submit' to their husbands? What does 'submit' mean in practical terms today?

Chapter 7

A PURPOSE IN RELATIONSHIPS

You may perhaps be familiar with this poem. In it two monkeys dialogue with one another (Darwin notwithstanding) about the impossibility of the human race having descended from their species.

DARWIN AND ALL THAT

Three monkeys sat in a coconut tree,
Discussing things as they're said to be.
Said one to the other, 'Now listen, you two,
There's a certain idea that can't be true:
That Man descended from our noble race.
Why, the very idea is a perfect disgrace!

No monkey ever deserted his wife,
Starved her babies and ruined her life;
And you've never known a mother monk
To leave her babies and do a bunk,
Or pass them on from one to another
Till they scarcely know who is their mother.

And another thing you'll never see –
A monk build a fence round a coconut tree
And let all the coconuts go to waste
Forbidding all other monks a taste.

Why, if I put a fence round a coconut tree
Starvation might force you to steal from me.

Here's another thing a monk won't do,
    Go out at night and get on a stew;
    Or use a gun, or club, or knife
    To take some other monkey's life!
Yes, Man's descended, the 'ornery cuss',
But brother, he didn't descend from us!'

Anonymous

Not only is it people in general who score badly on relationships issues, the same is all too often true of Christians.

One of the sad lessons we learn from Christian history is that churches and their members frequently find it very difficult to get on with one another. In fact they often spend their time bickering over non-essentials such as the church music, which version of the Bible to use, or pews versus chairs. Today in the United States alone there are 250 major denominations. Some of them represent genuine and sincerely held differences of opinion and have been founded in a gracious and conciliatory manner; but many have resulted from people's stubborn pig-headedness and a capacity to make a major issue out of what are in reality minor secondary issues.

Jesus prized unity between people, and especially his followers, very highly. In the famous often quoted prayer shortly before his crucifixion, Jesus prayed for all those who would believe in him:

... that all of them may be one, Father, just as you are in me and I am in you. May they also be in us so that the world may believe that you

have sent me. I have given them the glory that
you gave me, that they may be one as we are
one.

John 17:20–22

In the very early exhilarating days of the Christian
church, it was the bond of unity among the believers
which attracted so many to the Jesus they proclaimed.
The early chapters of Acts which chronicle these
events is sprinkled with phrases indicating the close
united relationships among the believers: 'All the
believers were together and had everything in
common' (Acts 2:44); 'All the believers were one
in heart and mind ... they shared everything they
had' (Acts 4:32). It is small wonder, therefore, that
Luke wrote: 'There were no needy persons among
them' (Acts 4:34) and that 'the Lord added to their
number daily' (Acts 2:47).

All through the New Testament we find Paul and
the other apostles urging Christians to be united
and at peace wih each other (Romans 12:16, 1 Corinthians 1:10–13):

> I appeal to you, brothers, in the name of our
> Lord Jesus Christ, that all of you agree with
> one another so that there may be no divisions
> among you and that you may be perfectly
> united in mind and thought. My brothers, some
> from Chloe's household have informed me that
> there are quarrels among you ... Is Christ
> divided?
>
> *1 Corinthians 1:10–13*

Paul went on to explain to the Christians in Corinth
that they, the individual members, were like the

different parts of a human body. They were all dependent on each other and all needed each other. For this reason they must 'be of one mind, live in peace' (2 Corinthians 13:11). Later when he wrote to the church at Philippi he pleaded with Euodia and Syntyche 'to agree with each other in the Lord' (Philippians 4:2). He also urged the whole congregation to be 'like-minded, having the same love, being one in spirit and purpose' (Philippians 2:2). He urged the Ephesian church to 'make every effort to keep the unity of the Spirit through the bond of peace' (Ephesians 4:3). James urged the churches he looked after to be 'peacemakers who sow in peace' and consequently 'raise a harvest of righteousness' (James 3:18). The apostle John urged the Christians to whom he wrote again and again to love one another and walk in love. So it's clear that God's purpose for all our relationships is that we should live with one another in peace and harmony. God's very nature is peace and harmony: unless Christians live in that same peace and harmony, not only will they not experience God's presence in their lives, but they will experience darkness and fear (1 John 4:16–18).

We are often slow to grasp this truth in our own personal lives and in our churches. We somehow imagine God is still going to bless us even when we are disagreeable, or promoters of discord. While openness is to be commended, there are people who think that a 'good dust up' with that other 'trying' individual will clear the air and solve the problem. There are misguided church committee members who think something can be achieved by stirring up the church meeting or sponsoring a disaffection campaign. There is too much truth in this parodied version of a verse from 'Onward Christian Soldiers'.

Like a mighty tortoise moves the Church of God,
Brothers, we are treading where we've always
trod.
We are all divided, many bodies we,
Very strong on doctrine, weak on charity.

Peter underlines God's purpose in relationships: there
is strength in union but only danger in discord. Such
danger could harm not only others, but equally, if not
more so, ourselves. Peter is no theorist. He sets out
five qualities in this section which can help us to
achieve this unity.

Finally, all of you, live in harmony with one
another; be sympathetic, love as brothers, be
compassionate and humble. Do not repay evil
with evil or insult with insult, but with blessing,
because to this you were called so that you may
inherit a blessing. For,

'Whoever would love life and see good days
must keep his tongue from evil and his lips from
deceitful speech.
He must turn from evil and do good; he must
seek peace and pursue it.
For the eyes of the Lord are on the righteous
and his ears are attentive to their prayer,
but the face of the Lord is against those who do
evil'.

1 Peter 3:3–12

Be sympathetic

Our English word 'sympathy' is derived from two
Greek words meaning 'to suffer' and 'with'. To be
sympathetic means to feel for another person to the

87

point where we, to some extent, enter into what they are going through. We tap into their pain, their hurt, their disappointment, their frustration.

Certain individuals are more sympathetic by nature; sometimes the reason for this is that they themselves have suffered in some measure. The capacity to offer real sympathy often comes as a result of our having felt the hurt of pain, disappointment and sorrow ourselves. We are told that Jesus was able to sympathise with us because he was 'tempted in every way, just as we are' (Hebrews 4:15). To be sympathetic may not come easily to many of us. It is not a quality we see much of in the twentieth century. Yet this is an ability which Peter urges us to cultivate in our relationships with people if we are going to live together in harmony.

Two things will help us to be more sympathetic towards others. One is to rid ourselves of our selfishness. As long as *our* agenda and *our* satisfaction is the most important thing, there is little hope that we will be able to put ourselves in another person's shoes. The other important aid to sympathy is to learn to be careful listeners. This means that we must concentrate on what the other person is telling us and resist the temptation to talk ourselves. Only in this way can the other person's feelings begin to make an impact on us. If we are Christians, to become more sympathetic is not quite as difficult as it might at first appear. Jesus is by his very nature sympathetic (or compassionate, if you prefer) and if we allow his Spirit to live in us he will make us more sensitive and feeling towards others. The apostle Paul summed up what it is to have sympathy for other people, in his letter to the church at Philippi: 'I have you in my heart' (Philippians 1:7).

My wife, Liz, has a life-long Ethiopian friend, Jember Tefera. Jember attended the same school in North Wales, did nursing training in London and later completed a research degree in health care at Manchester University. She is a relative of the late King Haile Selassie. Her husband was Mayor of Addis Ababa and Minister of Public Works. They lived in style and comfort in gracious surroundings. Following the Marxist-backed coup led by Mengistu in 1979 both Jember and her husband were political prisoners for five and eight and a half years respectively. From a life of ease and luxury Jember found herself having to share a flea-ridden mattress in a filthy, overcrowded prison cell. At first she was overcome with bitterness and very angry with God; but later she gave the whole situation completely over to him. Not only did she transform the prison by teaching hygiene, nursing care and reading, but when she was eventually discharged she was not bitter like so many others. In fact she emerged with a real sympathy for the poor. Nowadays she says that, through her experience, God has given her a heart for the poor.

Love as brothers

The word used is *philadelphoi*, *philia* being affection or love of a non-romantic kind. Philadelphia in the USA is the 'City of Brotherly Love' founded by Quaker emigrants. The notion of brotherly love goes back to the words of Jesus: 'My command is this: Love each other as I have loved you' (John 15:12). The New Testament is alarmingly explicit: 'We know that we have passed from death to life, because we love our brothers' (1 John 3:14). Just as it is usual to love and care for our earthly brothers and sisters, so we

89

should care and want the best for other members of the Christian community, who are part of the same family of God.

However, it does not automatically follow that, just because we are Christians, we are going to show practical care and love for others. It was Dostoevsky who recognised that 'loving everybody in general could easily become an excuse for loving nobody in particular'! Peter urges *all* of us to 'love as brothers'. Perhaps this is an appropriate moment for us to look at the level of our capacity to love others. Do we as individuals want to see others reach their full potential? Do we want to see a friend succeed, perhaps even where we have failed? This is what love demands of us. To love in this kind of way will involve us in giving our time, effort and emotional energy to others. It may involve us in visiting the sick and taking time to encourage those who cross our path who are down and discouraged. For many of us this will be a greater sacrifice than that of our money.

Be compassionate

What Peter is urging on us here is a quality quite close to the first quality he mentioned, namely sympathy or compassion. Compassion – or 'having a tender heart' as the word is translated in some versions of the Bible – is perhaps a more general virtue of being sensitively aware of people and situations of human need. It does not mean we actually share in other people's pain. When Bob Geldof was doing his epic race against time to help those who were dying of hunger, he said at one point that he was suffering from 'compassion fatigue'. It is very easy for any of us, when we are treated to a daily diet of war, homelessness and famine on our television screens, to become desensitised to human problems. One writer has commented:

> In our day . . . we have come too accustomed to
> hear of people's sufferings, and so tend to be
> superficially hardened and not easily or so
> deeply moved . . . There is all the more need
> for the free, fully and practical expression of
> such deep feeling among Christian brethren,
> issuing in corresponding action.

Many churches have become desensitised to a point
where they have lost the capacity to respond spon-
taneously in a tenderhearted, personal way. The
church's attitude has been described like this:

> I was hungry and you formed a committee to
> investigate my hunger. I was homeless and you
> filed a report on my plight. I was sick and
> you held a seminar on the situation of the
> underprivileged. You have investigated all
> aspects of my plight, and yet I am still hungry,
> homeless and sick.

There are a number of ways in which we can learn to
be more compassionate (or tender-hearted) in the way
that Peter urges us here. If we are compassionate, we
will be ready to make allowances for others and to
bend to the wishes of those who differ from us if the
situation demands it. We will also be more ready to
apologise to others and to forgive those who have
wronged us. 'Be kind and compassionate to one
another, forgiving each other, just as in Christ God
forgave you' (Ephesians 4:32).

We can make an effort to respond practically in
small ways when we see a situation which demands

a response. We can perhaps write a note of appreciation or give a small gift. We might express our compassion with some appropriate physical gesture, perhaps putting our hand on someone's shoulder or giving them a hug or kiss, or whatever is right for the particular situation. A physical gesture rightly made can be a very affirming and upbuilding experience. Jesus certainly gave such gestures to John 'the disciple he loved', and accepted them from Mary of Bethany and Mary of Magdala.

Our ability to be compassionate will grow in us in two ways. First, if we are Christians, Jesus, who is compassionate, lives in us by his Spirit and gradually will make us more sensitive to the needs of others. Second, as we consciously try to express compassion in our own lives we will grow to be more compassionate.

Be humble

Humility is distasteful to most Western men. It certainly does not fit the public school tradition and is out of keeping with the spirit of the armed forces and the world of sport. Muhammad Ali, the great heavyweight boxer, sometimes remarked, 'When you're as great as me it's difficult to be humble.'

One of the problems of our blowing up our own image like the Michelin Man is that it has the effect of cutting others down and leaving them feeling insignificant and undervalued. If we treat people in this kind of way then we are never going to be able to enter into a close, personal and harmonious relationship with them. Jesus claimed very few qualities for himself. Remarkably, one of the few he did claim was humility. 'Come to me,' he said, 'all you who are weary and burdened ... for I am gentle and humble in heart' (Matthew 11:28,29) In Jesus was 'all the full-ness of the Deity' (Colossians 2:9). Yet when he lived and worked in Judea, he didn't seek the limelight or play to the crowds. Rather, he took the form of a servant and made himself of no reputation (Philippians 2:6–7).

It is only as we approach other people on the same footing, knowing that they are equally valued and important to God, that we shall have any possibility of a close friendship based on mutual acceptance. This kind of true humility comes from, and is essentially, an inner attitude. As the third verse of the famous hymn, 'Come Down, O Love Divine', reads

> Let holy charity
> Mine outward vesture be,
> And lowliness become mine inner clothing;
> True lowliness of heart,
> Which takes the humble part,
> And o'er it own shortcomings weeps with
>   loathing.

Bianca da Siena, d. 1434

Basil Spence, in his book about the building of Coventry Cathedral, describes the occasion when he met Sir Jacob Epstein, the famous sculptor, who carved the figure of St Michael for the Cathedral. At the time Epstein was working on another figure and to Spence's surprise he asked for his comments. Spence, who knew nothing about sculpture at all, recalled, 'To my surprise he accepted my criticism immediately'. Spence wrote further:

> Like all great artists, he was fundamentally a
> humble man who would listen patiently to

anybody he respected. I have seen him take
serious note of the words of a child of nine
because, to quote Epstein, 'through innocence
you find truth'.

Perhaps we need to take stock and ask ourselves if
we are thinking of ourselves with a right estimate.
Are we humble towards others? More important, how
can we grow in humility? First, by recognising that,
however much we know, we know only a very little
compared with the total sum of knowledge. Equally,
however much we have achieved, it is in reality very
little. Above all, of course, we grow in humility by
keeping in constant touch with Jesus, the one who
embodied humility and lived a life of humility.

Bless those who mistreat you

We live in a world where the prevailing attitude is:
'He does me down so I do him down', or 'She speaks
unkind words about me so I'll poison her reputation
with gossip'. Yet Jesus' attitude was 'Bless those who
curse you, pray for those who ill-treat you.' Our
motive for forgiving someone who has wronged us is
that though we have wronged God and continue to
wrong him, he not only forgives us on account of
Jesus' sacrificial death, he continually pours out his
blessings on us. If we refuse to forgive someone else,
we are treating them more harshly than God does.
Furthermore, we need to forgive because if we do not,
we ourselves will suffer emotional hurt. If we are
always 'stewing' because of what someone else has
done to us, we are letting that person control our
emotions. They are spoiling our freedom to live and
relate even to those we love.

It is all too easy for us to bear grudges against

others in our family, or at work or church, towards another person who has misused or taken advantage of us. We should realise that the Lord does not hold anything against us, if we are genuinely sorry for it. The Lord not only forgives but he forgets as well! The story is told of a young man who gave into a particular temptation. He asked God to forgive him. Then just a short time later he succumbed another time. He said 'Lord, I'm so sorry, I've done it again.' The Lord said, 'Done what? I'm sorry, I've no recollection of your having done any such thing.' God does not remember wrongs that we have already asked forgiveness for, he forgives and forgets and so should we.

So we are to forgive those who mistreat us. In fact we are to do more than that, we are to bless such people: our aim should be to do something to positively benefit the person who mistreats us. This concept was a very familiar one to the Jews and Peter sums up the whole matter with an apt quotation from Psalm 34:12–16. If we want to bless others, we must 'keep [our] tongue[s] from evil' and 'seek peace', that is actively work to get things sorted out. And we must pray about any situation, because the Lord is attentive to our prayers. In fact Peter's quotation from Psalm 34 sums up the ways by which we can achieve God's purpose for all our relationships with other people. As we engage with others according to this prescribed pattern, we will discover the personal well-being, the richness and peace that come from close, happy personal relationships.

Discussion questions

1 Are there people you find particularly difficult to relate to? Why? Are there any ways that the presence of Christ in your life could change this?

2 Why are there disagreements and lack of unity in church congregations? How can lasting unity be created in your church or fellowship?

Chapter 8

A PURPOSE IN CHRISTIAN WITNESS

Just before his final departure back to the presence of his father, Jesus told his apostles:

> But you will receive power when the Holy Spirit comes on you; and you will be my witnesses in Jerusalem, in all Judea and Samaria, and to the ends of the earth.
>
> *Acts 1:8*

One of the most important reasons for our existence is that we should witness to other people about the change that Jesus has brought to our lives. Ulrich Zwingli, a reforming scholar along with Martin Luther and John Calvin, said, 'Nothing is of more concern to a man than to give account of his faith.' John Wesley, whose preaching brought a great revival to England in the eighteenth century, wrote *Twelve Rules* for his helpers. Rule 11 was: 'You have nothing to do but to save souls. Therefore spend and be spent in that work. And go always, not only to those who want you, but to those who want you most.' William Booth, founder of the Salvation Army, once visited King Edward VII. The monarch shook him warmly by the hand and said, 'You're doing a good work, a great work, General Booth.' The King then asked William Booth to pen a few lines in his autograph album. This is what he wrote:

> Your Majesty,
> Some men's ambition is art,
> Some men's ambition is fame,
> Some men's ambition is gold
> My ambition is the souls of men.

A witness, as we know from a courtroom, is simply someone who tells what he or she knows. Unfortunately, there are witnesses who tell 'the truth, the whole truth and nothing but the truth', and others who distort the truth, avoid the truth and deny the truth. The same is also the case with Christian witnesses. George Orwell wrote in his autobiographical novel *The Road to Wigan Pier*: 'As with the Christian religion, the worst advertisement for socialism is its adherents.'

For many the whole notion of Christian witness is a negative one. It reduces Christianity to the glitzy world of show biz and commercialism promoted by American televangelists. For others, it depersonalises and cheapens the Christian faith into a hard-sell package that can be pushed on people's doorsteps by smart young men in dark suits. For some 'witness' evokes far worse. It belongs to the world of cults with power-crazed womanising dictators who take people off and brainwash them with the Bible. In the popular mind and in many sections of the church the whole idea of witness smacks of fanaticism. It's David Koresh and Waco or Paul Berg and his Children of God.

But having acknowledged this to be the case, we must not be deterred simply because some people are behaving improperly. The way forward surely is not to abandon the practice altogether but to adopt the *right* practice. Peter lays out for us a number of guidelines to help us witness to our faith in Jesus in a way that will fulfil his purpose for us.

Be confident

> Who is going to harm you if you are eager to do good? But even if you should suffer for what is right, you are blessed. 'Do not fear what they fear; do not be frightened.' But in your hearts set apart Christ as Lord. Always be prepared to give an answer to everyone who asks you to give the reason for the hope that you have. But do this with gentleness and respect, keeping a clear conscience, so that those who speak maliciously against your good behaviour in Christ may be ashamed of their slander. It is better, if it is God's will, to suffer for doing good than for doing evil.
>
> *1 Peter 3:13–17*

'Do not fear what they fear; do not be frightened.' But in your hearts set apart Christ as Lord'. It is very easy when we meet our match to be tense and fearful. I spoke with one student who had come to the college where I teach to do a degree in Religious Studies. She said what an amazing experience it was to be able to talk to her lecturers freely about her Christian faith. At her school where she had done Religious Studies for 'A' level, she said she had been made to feel odd for being a Christian, even by her Religious

Studies teachers! I can still remember a time some ten or fifteen years past when I arrived in the staff room for coffee. Another colleague said, 'Sit down here, Nigel, with me because I'm going to explain to you why prayer is one hundred per cent useless.' He then went on to relate an incident which had been in the media all that week. A small child had fallen down a narrow well-shaft. People all around the world had prayed for her safe recovery. Finally after several days she had been taken out and was found to be dead. Prayer, it seemed, had accomplished nothing.

However, we are not to be afraid of what people say or might do to us. We see here how soaked Peter was in the Old Testament. When he writes this, he is drawing on the great promises of God:

> For I am the Lord, your God who takes hold of your right hand
> and says to you, Do not fear; I will help you.
>
> *Isaiah 41:13*

> Hear me, you who know what is right, you people who have my law in your hearts:
> Do not fear the reproach of men or be terrified by their insults.
>
> *Isaiah 51:7*

Throughout the Old Testament God's constant message to his people is 'Do not be afraid'. It comes particularly strongly in the books of Joshua, Isaiah and Jeremiah. I have heard it said that the words 'fear not' come 366 times in the Old Testament. That's one for every day of the year and one extra for leap years!

The writer of Hebrews in the New Testament reminds us that we can say with confidence, 'The Lord is my helper; I will not be afraid. What can man do to me?' (Hebrews 13:6).

I shall always remember Billy Graham arriving in England on the eve of one of his crusades. He was almost immediately escorted into a lounge to be interviewed by David Frost. Frost said, 'Now, Mr Graham, many hundreds of thousands of pounds have been spent on this crusade. Is it really going to be worth while?' Billy Graham replied, 'David, if I could just win you for Jesus Christ it would be all worth while!' The world is impressed by the likes of Billy Graham, Cliff Richard, or the MP David Alton, who are warm and confident about their Christian faith. Perhaps we might be tempted to think, 'Well, I'm not Billy Graham or Cliff Richard. I might put people off.' The fact of the matter is that they are 'put off' already and, provided we speak graciously, the chances are we might encourage someone.

At its roots 'fear' is lack of trust. If we fear, what we are saying is 'Lord, I can't trust you to see me through this. You're not big enough to help me'. Jesus once said to his disciples, 'You of little faith, why are you so afraid?' It was their lack of trust that caused them to fear. Paul reminds us that 'If God is for us, who can be against us?' We have also Jesus' great promise: 'And surely I am with you always, to the very end of the age' (Matthew 28:20).

The way to overcome our fears is to 'set apart Christ as Lord' in our hearts (1 Peter 3:15). We need to recognise that Jesus is ruling us and watching over us, so that if someone starts to question us or make fun of us because we are Christians, we can still remain confident in our witness.

Be courteous

Peter goes on to remind us that this confidence is to be tempered with courtesy: 'Always be prepared to give an answer to everyone who asks you to give the reason for the hope that you have. But do this with gentleness and respect'.

Some years ago someone wrote in large letters on the wall of Balliol College, Oxford 'Jesus is the answer'. Underneath a local wit added 'What's the question?' The problem sometimes is that we are either answering questions which people are not asking, or we are not answering courteously. Rather we give sermons or speak in incomprehensible 'God talk'. At other times God's people, his chosen people, can become his 'frozen' people, frozen at the mouth, that is. It's natural when we are put on the spot to put our head inside our defensive shell like a tortoise and excuse ourselves along the lines of 'My religion is personal' or 'My faith is a private matter just between myself and God'.

Peter hadn't always been able to answer for his faith in Jesus; he even denied him three times (Matthew 26:69–75). Nevertheless, he now urges that Christians 'always be prepared to give an answer to everyone who asks'. This means, of course, that we need to set aside a little time to make sure we know the important basics of the Christian faith: that Jesus was God in all his fullness, come as a human being into this world so that we could know him; that Jesus lived a perfect exemplary and selfless life; that he died as the perfect sacrifice through which we can receive God's forgiveness; that he came back to life so that all who want to can have a personal friendship with him; and that the Holy Spirit was sent so that we could experience God's presence and power in our lives.

However, we need to look at verse 15 carefully. It says we should have 'an answer'. We may not know all the necessary stuff but that doesn't matter. You can win the argument or give an overpowering answer and still lose the person. The important thing, and it is something we can all do, is to tell what Jesus is doing for *us*.

We can say, 'I am sorry I haven't got the answer to that but I can tell you that Jesus helped me with this.' 'He's enabled me to be more patient and understanding.' 'He's given my life a sense of direction and a goal to strive for.' 'I have sensed that he's there in my life and is guiding me.' 'He's helped me to stop holding grudges and to be more forgiving.'

Charles Studd was a name on every undergraduate and schoolboy's lips in the later part of the nineteenth century. He was England's cricket captain and a practising Christian. But in later times, when he looked back on these earlier days, he regretted his unwillingness to speak of his faith in Jesus. He wrote: 'Instead of going and telling others of the love of Christ I was selfish and kept the knowledge to myself. The result was that gradually my love began to grow cold, the love of the world came in.'

So we must be ready to give an answer, but it must be courteously and graciously given. It's to be done, says Peter, 'with gentleness and respect'. We need gentleness to try and understand someone asking a question. A question on suffering may not be a red-herring or self-defence; the person might be genuinely troubled by a trauma or a terminal illness. Christians are often very bad at listening. It has been rightly said that 'more people could be won for Christ if Christians spoke less not more!' And not only do we need to reply gently, we need to do it with respect, especially if we're speaking to someone older than we are. I can still remember being in a class on Western Value Systems at university. One member of the group, John, was an extreme fundamentalist who talked with great earnestness about Christianity. He was not always very sensitive. The professor said at the end of his paper, 'Well, John, we haven't heard from you today in our discussion.' John said, 'No, I am not interested in your puny little man-centred system of ethics.' He may have been right about the professor's ethics but his arrogance showed no respect. It says of Jesus in Luke's Gospel that 'all spoke well of him and were amazed at the gracious words that came from his lips' (Luke 4:22).

Review your conscience

Conscience has often been defined as 'the voice of God in man'. Generally speaking it is a reliable guide as to what is right and wrong in your life although it is possible for conscience to be conditioned. Martin Luther said that 'to go against conscience is neither safe nor right.' And it will probably follow that if we avoid anything which goes against the dictates of 'a clear' conscience the quality of our lives will be such that people are attracted to Christ and take notice of our faith (v16).

In the last analysis, the witness that convinces another person of the reality of Jesus is the quality of our total life, thought, attitudes and behaviour. Dr Rhadakrishnan, a Hindu philosopher and former president of India, is said to have commented to some Christians: 'You claim that Jesus Christ is your saviour, but you do not appear to be more saved than anyone else.'

We can be the most handsome or beautiful person and skilled in debate but, if *who* we are gives a different signal, we won't carry any weight or influence. A year or so ago I heard someone recount the story of a Christian university student. He was surrounded by noisy people who kept anti-social hours. His immediate neighbour played very loud music and often came home drunk. This Christian lad didn't socialise. He only went to Christian meetings. One day in the second term his neighbour said, 'Would you like to come in for a cup of coffee?' When he got into the guy's room suddenly a whole term and half's worth of frustration and anger about the noise and the late night banging and clatter took hold of him. He just let rip with the most incredible venom. When he had finished, his neighbour said, 'I'm really sorry but you see my mother's just died and you're the only Christian I know and I wondered if you could help me.'

Remember Christ

> For Christ died for sins once for all, the righteous for the unrighteous, to bring you to God. He was put to death in the body but made alive by the Spirit, through whom also he went and preached to the spirits in prison who disobeyed long ago when God waited patiently in the days of Noah while the ark was being built. In it only a few people, eight in all, were saved through water, and this water symbolises baptism that now saves you also – not the removal of dirt from the body but the pledge of a good conscience towards God. It saves you by the resurrection of Jesus Christ, who has gone

into heaven and is at God's right hand – with
angels, authorities and powers in submission to
him.

1 Peter 3:18–22

Suffering Christians have drawn strength to continue
their witness by remembering Jesus and what he suffered on their behalf. Stephen, the first Christian
martyr, died calling on Jesus for strength (Acts 7:59).
Christians suffering under the cruel hand of the
Roman Emperor were sustained by Jesus 'the Lamb,
who was slain' (Revelation 5:12).

John Bunyan, the Bedford tinker, was arrested in
November 1660 by a local magistrate for preaching
in the fields. He refused to give an undertaking not
to continue and was imprisoned off and on for the
next twelve years. Much of the courage which he
showed during that time he gained quite simply from
fixing his thoughts and attentions on Jesus. He
recounted his own story in allegorical form in his most
famous book, *Pilgrim's Progress*. Central to the book is
coming to the cross where the burden that he had
carried was rolled away from him.

Jesus experienced opposition far more harsh than
most of us are ever likely to encounter, yet he did not
react ungraciously or violently; he entrusted himself
to the Father. Jesus is the supreme example of a person
suffering unjust opposition. He was the perfect spot-
less Lamb of God (John 1:29) 'the righteous' as Peter
calls him in verse 18; yet he allowed himself to be put
to death on a cross so that all the wrong in our lives
can be taken away and we can know God. So, when
we are up against it, we need to remember Jesus and
what he went through for us. This, says Peter, will
help to sustain us when we feel the hassle or the

pressure on us is too much to cope with:

> Let us fix our eyes on Jesus ... who ... endured
> the cross, scorning it's shame ...
>
> *Hebrews 12:2*

I have often found it a help to picture Jesus in my mind when the going gets hard. I visualise his kind caring face, using my memory of a lighted picture which stands behind the communion table of the church that I attended up until the time I was married. I find it helps me to keep up my relationship with Jesus and to be in touch with him in prayer.

In verses 19 and 20, Peter digresses a little in his thought about the sufferings of Jesus on our behalf. Not only did Jesus suffer a cruel and unjust death, he had to go to the very place of the dead inhabited by the wicked who had rejected God out of their own wilful disobedience. To these spirits Jesus proclaimed his triumph over sin and death. This victory is pictured by the ceremony of Christian baptism, which also symbolises Jesus' death and resurrection. When a person is baptised, their plunging under the water is a symbolic picture of Jesus' death and burial and their identification with it. Equally the baptised person's emergence up out of the water reminds them that Jesus has overcome suffering and death.

The paragraph ends on a note of real encouragement. The Jesus who suffered the pain and humility of a criminal death is now not only alive again, he is in the place of power at God's right hand. To put it simply, Jesus is now in the position where he can both watch over us and give us the strength to enable us to maintain our witness for him.

Change your behaviour

Therefore, since Christ suffered in his body, arm
yourselves also with the same attitude, because
he who has suffered in his body is done with
sin. As a result, he does not live the rest of his
earthly life for evil human desires, but rather for
the will of God. For you have spent enough
time in the past doing what pagans choose to
do – living in debauchery, lust, drunkenness,
orgies, carousing and detestable idolatry. They
think it strange that you do not plunge with them
into the same flood of dissipation, and they heap
abuse on you. But they will have to give
account to him who is ready to judge the living
and the dead. For this is the reason the gospel
was preached even to those who are now dead,
so that they might be judged according to men
in regard to the body, but live according to
God in regard to the spirit.

1 Peter 4:1–6

Peter finally rounds off this section about Christian
witness by underlining the need for right conduct.
Christians, he says, are committed to abandon the
ways of 'pagans'. It was said of the philosopher Plato
that 'his deeds matched his words and his words
matched his deeds'. Christians have got to follow suit
if our witness is to count for anything in the eyes of
other people.

In particular, Peter mentions 'debauchery, lust,
drunkenness, orgies, carousing and detestable idolatry'. Quite why these particular instances of miscon-
duct have been singled out in verse 3 is not clear. It
may simply be that these typified the behaviour of

some of his readers in the days before they became Christians. Clearly any kind of behaviour that dishonours God's name must be eradicated from our lives. Sometimes it may not be an easy issue to decide. I remember once being offered this guideline: if you would be glad to be met by Jesus while engaging in a particular activity, it is probably one he would approve of. Our conduct has got to be influenced not by our 'evil human desires' but rather by 'the will of God'.

The famous Dr Johnson once said, 'You can tell a man by the company he keeps.' Peter makes the same point. If we are Christians, part of our witness will be to avoid the company of those who are 'wild and reckless' (v4, GNB) in their living. For sure some may sneer at us as 'narrow minded' and 'puritanical'; others no doubt will give us a mouthful of 'abuse'; but the apostle concludes by reminding us of the coming day of judgement when everyone, the living and the dead, will have to give an account of their conduct to Jesus, the righteous judge.

When John Bunyan turned his life over to Jesus, he was marvellously changed. 'Yea,' said Bunyan, 'young and old for a while had some reformation in them; also some of them perceiving that God had mercy on me came crying to him for mercy too.' Peter urges us to ensure that our Christian witness may have a similar impact on those who interact with us and cross our paths from day to day.

Discussion questions

1 Do you find it hard to speak to others about your Christian faith?
2 If a stranger asked you to tell them what mattered to you most in life, what would you say?

Chapter 9

A PURPOSE IN OUR GIFTS AND ABILITIES

The end of all things is near. Therefore be clear minded and self-controlled so that you can pray. Above all, love each other deeply, because love covers over a multitude of sins. Offer hospitality to one another without grumbling. Each one should use whatever gift he has received to serve others, faithfully administering God's grace in its various forms. If anyone speaks, he should do it as one speaking the very words of God. If anyone serves, he should do it with the strength God provides, so that in all things God may be praised through Jesus Christ. To him be the glory and the power for ever and ever. Amen.

1 Peter 4:7–11

I have vivid and happy memories of spending some Christmases at my parents-in-law's rambling Suffolk rectory. Often the house would be full with my wife's brothers and their children. On one occasion there were twenty-one of us in all, parents, grandparents and children. The after-dinner ritual consisted of going into the sitting room to an enormous stack of presents. They were all different in size and value but there was something for everyone, probably more than most of us needed!

In a small way this is a pale reflection of how things are in God's family. Every single one of us, young or old, has been given and entrusted with at least one gift or ability by God our Father (1 Corinthians 12:7; Matthew 25:15). Part of God's purpose for us is that we should enjoy using whatever gifts and abilities we have been given not just for our own satisfaction but in order to benefit and enrich others. The gifts and abilities to which Peter refers are part of a wide range, which we find listed in various places in the New Testament. Very roughly, we can put them into three groups: gifts of speaking, gifts of action and gifts of knowledge.

• *Gifts of speaking* There is the gift of tongues which is a prayer language that enables the believer to worship God in greater depth and with greater release of the inner emotions. There is prophecy of which Paul speaks in detail in 1 Corinthians 14. To prophesy is to speak for the 'strengthening, encouragement and comfort' of other people. There are also the important speaking gifts of teaching, preaching and evangelism.
• *Action gifts* include healing, the working of miracles, administration, the giving of money, helping or practical care.
• *Gifts of knowledge* These include 'knowledge', 'wisdom' and 'discernment'. Knowledge is a God-given disclosure of something which could not normally be known. Jesus demonstrated that he had this gift when he knew that the woman he met with in the Samaritan town of Sychar had had five husbands

(John 4:4–42). Wisdom is the ability to counsel rightly; and discernment is the ability to distinguish whether something is from God or not.

There are always some individuals who have the view that their gifts are either of very limited worth or non-existent. However, the New Testament is emphatically clear that this is not so (eg Matthew 25:14–30). We all have something to offer. The problem very often is that we are not satisfied with the particular gifts that we have, or we only want the more spectacular ones like public speaking and working miracles. When we think of our gifts, it is perhaps good to remember the following points that Peter is making.

The reason for using our gifts and abilities
'The end of all things is near.' This theme runs right through the New Testament (Romans 13:12; Philippians 4:5; James 5:8; 1 John 2:18; Revelation 3:11). It has been estimated that one out of every ten verses in the New Testament make some reference either directly or indirectly to the return of Jesus and 'the end of all things'.

As we ponder these texts and others like them, we may wonder why nearly 2000 years have come and gone and the end has still not arrived. Part of the answer is that, we are living in the period which lies between Jesus' first coming and his second and final coming, which will take place at the end of human history as we now know it. The apostles referred to this period as 'the last days'. On the day of Pentecost, when the Holy Spirit was poured out on the church, Peter declared it a sign of 'the last days'(Acts 2:1–36). The writer of the letter to the Hebrews wrote that 'in these last days [God] has spoken to us by his Son' (Hebrews 1:2).

Looked at from God's perspective, the time factor has no relevance. As the psalmist put it, 'a thousand years in your sight are like a day that has just gone by, or like a watch in the night' (Psalm 90:4). Later Peter echoed these very words (2 Peter 3:8). Seen in this way the word 'near' can cover centuries.

There is another personal sense in which for everyone of us the 'end of all things is near'. The one certain thing is that all of us will die. As George Bernard Shaw once put it: 'Death is the ultimate statistic: one out of one dies'. For everyone of us in this sense, the Lord is near.

The Lord is coming soon. If we knew for an absolute certainty that Jesus was scheduled to make his final re-appearance on this earth on Tuesday next week, we would all be hard at it aiming to get as many things sorted out as possible in a short space of time!

Dwight L Moody, the nineteenth century American evangelist, said there were three things which completely changed his Christian living. The first was when he started to tell others about Jesus. The second was when he was filled by the Holy Spirit. The third was his arrival at the conviction that Jesus would return to this earth. The expectation that Jesus could return at any point in time, perhaps even when we least expect it (Matthew 24:36–51), should motivate us to use to the full the gifts which God has given us. And when he does come, we will find ourselves answerable to the Lord who is the giver of all the gifts and abilities we possess.

It doesn't seem to matter what gifts and abilities we have, it is always possible to misuse them for our own ends or to harm other people. On a purely human level charisma and ability in public speaking can be used to benefit thousands. We have only to think of the positive influence of people such as John Wesley, Mahatma Ghandi or Archbishop Desmond Tutu, to recognise this. On the other hand, the same gift used by Adolf Hitler or Joseph Stalin can result in hideous inhumanity and wickedness. Equally charm and beauty can be used to inspire and delight or to manipulate and control people. The same possibility is there in all the gifts (v10) that God has given for use by his church. They have the potential to benefit, encourage and help others; but they can also cause hurt and do great damage. The church at Corinth was blessed with many gifted members (1 Corinthians 1:7). Sadly, their gifts became the basis of factions and quarrels (1 Corinthians 1:11–13). It is for this reason that Peter gives us advice on the way we should use our gifts and abilities.

How to use our gifts and abilities

Peter offers us four guidelines that will enable us to use our gifts and abilities in an effective, positive and helpful way.

First of all, he suggests that we *use them sanely*. He writes: 'be clear-minded' (v7) The word means literally 'to keep your mind safe'. To be sane means not being swept along by sudden enthusiasms or prone to unbalanced fanaticism.

One of the things which distinguishes us as human beings is that we have been created with minds. We can, unlike the animal world, make our own conscious decisions. We are exhorted by Jesus to love God with all our minds (Matthew 22:37). This doesn't mean that we don't accept anything unless we can bend our minds round it. Thankfully God is greater than our minds! It does mean, however, that we use our rational sense where our Christian faith is concerned. It is still good that we question things and think carefully about the consequences of our actions. It's all too easy to simply act on someone else's advice or guidance, or take some course of action on the spur of the moment in response to 'a word' someone alleges has come direct from God! Every course of action needs to be tested out against the principles of the Bible's teaching. It has been wisely said 'the devil is always in a hurry'. God's people need to take time to think things over carefully and reach a sensible decision. Sadly it's Christians who don't keep a hold on their minds who sometimes end up in a Waco or a Jonestown community. The point of all of this is that if we don't consider matters thoughtfully, people who are a part of our church or Christian group could so easily get hurt or damaged.

Peter also urges us to use our gifts and abilities *soberly*. The New International Version translates this as 'self-controlled' (v7). The word was first used to mean being sober as opposed to being drunk. Later in New Testament times, it came to mean 'to act soberly and sensibly'. This does not mean that a Christian must be lost in gloom and misery. It does, however, require that our approach to life must be responsible and sensible in terms of our daily conduct.

When it comes to the use of our gifts and abilities there are plenty of Christians who 'go over the top' and put on their own private show, particularly where gifts of teaching, preaching and speaking are concerned. Bishop Ryle of Liverpool in the last century once said in reference to the power of the Holy Spirit, 'There are few people who can hold a full cup with a steady hand.' So, if our gifts are public in nature we need to take particular care to use them soberly. Movements of Holy Spirit renewal have brought a great deal of healing and help to the Christian churches. They have enabled Christians to experience the presence of Jesus in their own lives in greater depth and in a personal way. This has meant that their conversion experience has been more than mere mental acceptance of Bible teaching and the doctrine of creeds. All of this is good but we need to take care that we keep a balance in our behaviour.

In the early Christian church in Asia Minor (modern Turkey) in the second century, a group of Christians followed Montanus, a man of high standards of behaviour who practised fasting and self-discipline. He also stressed the importance of prophecy. Sadly, instead of following Paul's directions that prophets must always be in control of themselves (1 Corinthians 14:32), he appears to have taught his followers that they had to get into a frenzied state before they could prophesy. In more recent times the church has witnessed a variety of colourful behaviour. A J Tomlinson, one of the founders of the Church of God, used often to spend much of the services on the floor of his place of worship, screaming. Other obvious instances of unbalanced behaviour include such things as the excesses of American televangelism and the moral collapses of some of its leading personalities; or the over-emphasis on doing battle with the demonic as practised by certain charismatic groups. However, Peter is telling us that if we are going to benefit others by our gifts and activities we have got to live and act as normal, rational human beings.

A third guideline which Peter brings before us if we want to use our gifts effectively is *prayer*. In all that we do, we want, above everything else, to have God's perspective. This means that we must keep in constant touch with him by praying continually (1 Thessalonians 5:17). In short Peter is urging us to preserve our prayer life.

It takes time and effort to keep any relationship alive and vital. This is made all the more demanding by the pressures of living. Our relationship with Jesus is no different. We have to set aside time to be with him and share our concerns with him. Martin Luther used to say, 'If you are too busy to pray, you really are too busy.' Someone else has said, 'The measure of our belief in prayer is the time that we actually spend in it.' Do we need to rearrange our daily timetable to make adequate time for prayer? It is a fact that we can't *find* time; we have to *make* it.

Studies have shown that churches which are 'going' churches have a deep commitment to prayer. The same is true of individual Christians. None of us can expect to live effectively as Christians, let alone help other people with our gifts and abilities, without regular daily prayer. In particular, we need to pray for those in our fellowship who we want to help and encourage.

'*Above all, love each other deeply*' (v8). The word which Peter uses to describe love has two meanings: 'constant' in the sense of unchanging or never failing; and 'stretching' like a runner straining himself to the full as he nears the finishing tape. Christian love, as we are doubtless aware, is not primarily a feeling or sentiment, it's an act of our will as we consciously make an effort to reach out to the difficult and the needy and those with problems.

Sandwiched in between chapter 12 and chapter 14 of Paul's first letter to the Corinthians, is the famous chapter 13 which deals with the necessity of love. What Paul is in effect saying is this: it doesn't matter how many gifts and abilities we have unless we use them in a loving way, they will benefit no one. Love, he reminds us, is patient, gentle and kind. It isn't boastful, or self-seeking; it protects, trusts and perseveres. If we utilise our gifts and abilities in this kind of way the results will be widespread and positive.

Love is a very powerful thing: 'It 'covers over a multitude of sins'. If we love, we will be ready to forgive others. It is as we forgive that God also forgives us and our sins are taken from his view. The prophet Isaiah spoke of God blotting out our sins (Isaiah 43:25). There is also another sense in which 'love covers over a multitude of sins'. We may have our individual faults but, if we are people who are always kind, sympathetic and warm, if we're forgiving and not condemning, that love will be what will save a situation. This does not mean we pretend we have not been wronged by others. If love is sufficiently broad and big hearted, it will cover over, at least from our conscious thoughts, the wrong in our situations. It has rightly been said, 'Loving someone is caring and wanting the best for them. If we really love a person we'll be aware of their faults but much more ready to overlook them and try again with them.'

Using our gifts and abilities

Having given some basic guiding principles as to how we should use our gifts, Peter now moves on to write about the practice itself. Clearly there are a great many gifts and it is clear that whatever our particular strengths, we should use them to the full. For this reason Peter mentions three which are common to almost all of us: hospitality, speaking and practical service.

Hospitality

Without hospitality the early church could not have existed. The first missionaries to spread the good news needed places in which to stay. Because inns were few and far between in the Roman Empire and often immoral places, the only accommodation available in many cases were Christian homes. In addition to this, up until the third century there were no official church buildings, and congregations met for worship and other activities in people's houses. Hospitality was therefore the major basis on which the early church spread. Significantly, the church's missionary work was never more effective than in that first early phase.

It's interesting to reflect that the largest church in the world, the Yoi Do Full Gospel Church in Seoul, Korea, pastored by Paul Yongi Cho, is founded on hospitality. There are ninety thousand small groups which meet in people's homes every week. Each group has about twelve to fourteen members. Many of them are led by women who have more time in the day to get discussions planned and organised. Perhaps one of the factors in the wonderful success of this church is that they have understood the New Testament emphasis on hospitality. The home is often the place where people who are strangers to the Christian faith feel most relaxed and are most ready to open up. Perhaps as churches and as individuals we need to ask ourselves whether we are fulfilling one of God's purposes in our homes, that is the giving of hospitality.

Hospitality is something which the New Testament urges all Christians to practice. This means not just entertaining our close friends but also from time to time looking beyond to the needs of others. Jesus commended those who welcomed people they did not know into their homes (Matthew 25:35). The writer of the letter to the Hebrews commended the practice of giving hospitality to strangers because by this means 'some ... have entertained angels without knowing it' (Hebrews 13:2). Paul similarly urged the Christians in Rome to 'share with God's people who are in need. Practise hospitality' (Romans 12:13). And here Peter tells us to offer hospitality to others 'without grumbling' (v9).

Speaking
'If anyone speaks, he should do it as one speaking the very words of God' (v11). Peter isn't referring specifically to preaching although he obviously includes it. The important thing, he says, is that whether we preach, teach or prophesy or simply speak to a neighbour, that we do it in such a way that we bring them into direct touch with God.

Some years ago I read a book written by Carlos Ortiz, *The Cry of the Human Heart*. Ortiz was making the point that when people come to a place of worship on Sunday they do not just want to hear a passage from the Bible; they want to hear what God is saying to them on that particular day and in a particular situation or particular need. It's perfectly possible to go to a church service and hear a passage explained, but it's not really what the Lord wants to say: it lacks reality. What the human heart cries for Ortiz says, is 'the living word'.

Someone was telling me of an American pastor who has learnt and thought over literally hundreds of Bible verses. He does this so that whenever he's with someone who needs a word of encouragement he can quietly wait on God's Holy Spirit to bring into his mind some part of God's word which will exactly fit

121

the need.

Speaking is a gift is shared by many Christians. We won't have all the answers to questions about the Christian faith or to the ultimate issues of life such as suffering and injustice. Nevertheless, we do all have the potential to help and encourage others by the things we say.

Practical service
Any Christian engaged in Christian service 'should do it with the strength God provides'. The word 'serves' refers to the practical expression of Christian love such as feeding the hungry, caring for the sick, the refugees and the hungry. Leonard Bernstein, the famous conductor, was once asked, 'What is the most difficult instrument to play?' He replied, 'Second fiddle.' There are plenty of people willing to take a lead, but not so many who are willing to serve in smaller ways. Perhaps this is another area where we need to take a fresh look at ourselves. Are we willing to lend a hand to do a job, to give a neighbour a ride, to do a little cooking when someone is ill?

'To him be the glory . . .'
The aim or purpose of our using our gifts and abilities is 'so that in all things God may be praised'. Interestingly the motto of the great Benedictine order of monks is 'I GOD' which stands for the Latin words *In omnibus glorificatur Deus*: 'In all things may God be glorified'. The word 'glory' means 'reflected brightness'. Just as the moon has no light of its own but simply reflects the brightness of the sun, so our aim must be that all we do – welcoming, speaking or caring – may reflect 'the glory and the power' of God. Amen!

An example of what can result when Christians use

their gifts to the full is the coming into being of the Harnhill Centre for Christian Healing in 1986. Harnhill is a peaceful Cotswold village on the outskirts of Cirencester. It all began in 1984 when Canon Arthur Dodds and his wife Letty were lunching at Harnhill Manor which was then the home of Robert and Mary Henley. Discovering that they were thinking of selling Arthur chanced the remark, 'What a wonderful centre of Christian healing your home would make!' So it proved.

Over the next two years Arthur mobilised people to pray and a management committee was set up to raise the £300,000 which was needed. At the same time people with a whole variety of gifts and talents were brought together. One individual headed up the buildings programme and a retired accountant in his seventies became treasurer. A lively Christian lady headed up the publicity. Another lady, a 'very slow reader', took on the bookstall. In October 1984 a young teacher felt that God was telling her to leave teaching and 'go and work full-time for him'. She did so and eventually found her way to Harnhill where her leadership in music became an inspiration. By October 1986 a resident staff was in place led by Hugh and Hilary Kent whose gifts of welcoming love and pastoral care have blessed so many.

The centre is now vibrant with life. Today visitors from all over the country come to one of the twice weekly healing services, or stay for a few days quiet rest and refreshment to enjoy the delights of the beautiful Gloucestershire countryside. People report depression lifted, cancers healed and their hopes rekindled. Here is a place where God is indeed being praised as a result of people using the gifts which he has entrusted to them.

Discussion questions

1 Make a list of the things you are best at and enjoy most. Are there ways in which you can develop these talents?

2 Some people say that the gifts of the Holy Spirit mentioned in the New Testament were only for the lifetime of the apostles. Do you agree? Write down those gifts which you think should be seen in today's church.

Chapter 10

A PURPOSE IN SUFFERING

Dear friends, do not be surprised at the painful trial you are suffering, as though something strange were happening to you. But rejoice that you participate in the sufferings of Christ, so that you may be overjoyed when his glory is revealed. If you are insulted because of the name of Christ, you are blessed, for the Spirit of glory and of God rests on you. If you suffer, it should not be as a murderer or thief or any other kind of criminal, or even as a meddler. However, if you suffer as a Christian, do not be ashamed, but praise God that you bear that name. For it is time for judgment to begin with the family of God; and if it begins with us, what will the outcome be for those who do not obey the gospel of God? And,

'If it is hard for the righteous to be saved, what will become of the ungodly and the sinner?'

So then, those who suffer according to God's will should commit themselves too their faithful Creator and continue to do good.

1 Peter 4:12–19

At this point we come face to face with the sufferings that a number of the people Peter was writing to were actually experiencing at the hands of the pagan Roman government. Some of them, it seems, were being made to suffer like murderers and other common criminals simply because they were Christians. On occasion there may have been the opportunity to give a reason for their Christian faith but here this clearly isn't the case. Their only hope was to trust in God. Some of the Roman governors were unable to find any crimes associated with Christians who lived in their provinces, so they resorted to execution without trial. One of their number, Pliny, who was governor of the province of Bythinia at the end of the first century, acted in just this kind of way. He wrote to the Roman Emperor, Trajan, and explained his policy as follows:

> This is the course I have adopted in the case of those brought before me as Christians. I ask them if they are Christians. If they admit it I repeat the question a second and a third time, threatening capital punishment; if they persist I sentence them to death. For I do not doubt that, whatever kind of crime it may be to which they have confessed, their pertinacity and inflexible obstinacy should be punished.

This kind of cruel torture and bitter hardship is something which has been repeated many times down through Christian history. The twentieth century has witnessed brutal treatment meted out by the Stalin and Kruschev regimes in the Soviet Union. Thousands of Christians ended their days in Siberian labour camps or simply disappeared, their deaths unmarked and unrecorded. In Germany in the Second World War Dietrich Bonhoeffer was imprisoned and eventually executed as a result of his resistance to Adolf Hitler. While he was in prison Bonhoeffer wrote:

> It is infinitely easier to suffer in obedience to a human command than to suffer in the freedom of an act undertaken purely on one's own responsibility. It is infinitely easier to suffer in community than to suffer in loneliness ... Christ suffered in freedom, in loneliness, apart and in shame, in body and in spirit, and many Christians have since suffered with him.

In more recent years there have been many similar examples of heartless brutality being handed out to Christians. In Uganda during the time of President Idi Amin Christians suffered and the Archbishop, Janani Luwum, cruelly murdered. Christians in the Sudan have been the victims of many atrocities in the 1980s and 1990s. This fact was highlighted by the Archbishop of Canterbury's brave and welcome visit to the south of the country in the early part of 1994. Persecution at this kind of level is something which people in Britain have not had to face. Nevertheless, for some it's not an easy thing to be loyal to Jesus on the factory floor, or in the office, the barracks, school or college. Suffering is something which is common to all Christians.

It is sometimes hard to make any sense at all out of suffering. Aldous Huxley called it 'The Riddle of the Universe'. Why natural disasters should happen, and why a good and loving God should allow illness, cruelty, pain or torture – for example, the phyical abuse of an innocent child – is beyond the limits of human understanding. Perhaps in the end, we can only begin to make sense of suffering in two ways. First, God did not create robots. He made human beings with the ability to make choices. Man's inhumanity to man results from choosing the wrong course of action. The blame for cruelty, violence and abuse cannot therefore be laid on God's doorstep. People sometimes say, 'Why doesn't God do something?' meaning why doesn't he intervene and put an end to evil and suffering? But how much do we want God to go on intervening? If he were to intervene in every single situation, all free choice would be gone. The human race would be reduced to mere automatons. Second, Christianity doesn't see God standing idly on the touchline. Rather, in Jesus he came and shared in human suffering to show how we should handle it in our own lives. As the Russian philosopher, Nicolai Berdyaev, put it: 'We can only reconcile ourselves to the tragedy of the world, because God suffers too.' Clearly Peter did not believe God to be the cause of human suffering and injustice any more than we do. Nevertheless, he saw that God can still work his purposes through human suffering.

To draw us closer to Christ

In verse 13, Peter writes that by trials we 'participate in the sufferings of Christ'. Christians suffer like everyone else because they live in a world inhabited by selfish people with a capacity for evil as well as for good. Yet Tertullian, one of the leaders of the Christian church in North Africa at the beginning of the third century, wrote: 'He who fears to suffer, cannot belong to him who suffered.' Jesus made it clear that to follow him was never going to be an easy thing:

> Remember the words I spoke to you: 'No servant is greater than his master.' If they persecute me, they will persecute you also ... They will treat you this way because of my name, for they do not know the One who sent me.'
>
> *John 15:20,21*

When we suffer and bear pain or hardship because we are Christians, we are walking in the way that Jesus walked, sharing the cross that Jesus carried. In that experience we therefore come close to Jesus himself. The Bible describes Jesus as 'a suffering servant' (Isaiah 52:13–53:12). After his resurrection he went back into his Father's presence, but he took with him the experience of the worst kinds of unjust suffering. For this reason, he still knows what it is to share the pain of human hurt and cruelty (Hebrews 4:15).

Richard Wurmbrand, a Rumanian pastor, was tortured for his Christian faith by the Communist authorities. He was in prison for a total of fourteen years. Among other atrocities, his captors fractured four vertebrae in his back and burnt and cut eighteen holes in his body. He had several spells in solitary confinement during which he was kept in a cold cell thirty feet below ground. Yet he found the presence of Jesus to be so close that at times he literally danced for joy.

Acts 3:11–4:31 relates how Peter, and some of the apostles, had been preaching in Solomon's Colonnade in Jerusalem. The Sanhedrin had them arrested and flogged. Luke reports that they left the authorities rejoicing because they had been considered worthy of suffering disgrace for the name of Jesus. Peter knew from experience that suffering for being Jesus' followers often brings his presence particularly near. The joy of which Peter speaks in verse 13 is not in the suffering; rather it is in the fact that the suffering we experience draws us closer to Christ.

Perhaps there is a word here for our encouragement. We may not have to cope with suffering of this kind but some of us may be in a situation where the going is hard. Perhaps we live in a home where others make light of our Christian faith, or resent our time spent in Christian concerns and activities. It may be that in our work place or college environment others are giving us stick for our commitment to Christian standards of behaviour. Again Christian people sometimes find themselves cornered by hostile questioning or passed over in the promotion stakes on account of their refusal to compromise on codes of conduct. In all of these situations it is part of God's purpose to draw us closer to himself and to his Son.

To show Christ's glory

It is through suffering that Christ's glory is seen more clearly in us. I am often impressed when I take glass dishes out of the dishwasher, which perhaps isn't as often as I should! When they are put in, they are caked with the remains of food; but when they are washed and taken out, they literally sparkle as a result of the combination of hot water, salt and rinsing agent. The trials, difficulties and suffering which we experience are in some ways like the hot water in the dishwasher: they have a purifying effect on us. If we cling to our relationship with Jesus in these times, then his presence will be seen in us more clearly. Peter actually uses the word 'glory' in the text.

The Jews referred to this as the Shekina: the luminous glow of the presence of God. There are a number of places in the Old Testament where individuals and groups of God's people saw this special presence of God (Exodus 16:7,10; 24:15–17; 29:42,43; 1 Kings 8:10,11). The appearance of the intense brightness of God's glorious presence recurs frequently in the Old Testament. The same glowing presence of God came on Jesus at his transfiguration (Matthew 17:1, 2).

Peter encourages us with the fact that the glory of Jesus rests on the person who suffers. As we reflect on the lives of some Christians who have suffered a great deal we can see this truth illustrated. During his lifetime John Bunyan endured many trials and conflicts. As a result of his suffering, God's glory rested on Bunyan in a remarkable way. J C Lawson, one of his biographers, wrote: 'Sometimes he was so overwhelmed with the sense of God's grace and power that he could hardly bear up under it.'

To strengthen our faith in Christ

It's the way in which we react when under pressure or experiencing difficulties that reveals our true colours.

One of the students at the college where I teach was an army officer who had been seconded to take a degree in English and Religious Studies. He related how on one occasion he had been sent on an extremely arduous operation as part of their training in battle discipline. For three days and nights they were kept constantly on the go. They had to carry a heavy pack. They were not allowed to sleep and rest stops were limited. At the end of that time they were taken into a simulated battle area with low flying aircraft, tanks and machine guns and put through their paces. The whole purpose of the operation was, first of all, to test what they were capable of, but it also had the additional function of toughening them up and making them stronger and better soldiers with more stamina and a greater capacity for endurance.

Peter sees the suffering and trials which we may experience as Christians as fulfilling a similar role. As Paul put it in his letter to Timothy, 'everyone who wants to live a godly life in Christ Jesus will be persecuted' (2 Timothy 3:12). But in addition, suffering can also have the effect of strengthening our commitment to Jesus.

Georgi Vins, one of the leaders of the underground Baptist church in Soviet Russia in the 1960s, wrote movingly of his suffering in his autobiography. The Vins family encountered bitter opposition and hostility for their faith. When Georgi was a little lad, his father, Peter Vins, was imprisoned for his Christian activities. Georgi recalled how he used to kneel at his bedside with his mother and repeat just four words: 'Jesus! Bring Daddy back.' Georgi himself was later in prison almost continuously from 1967 for more than fifteen years. Yet for all their suffering, the one thing that emerged from this account is that the faith of the persecuted Soviet Christians not only remained intact, it was deepened and strengthened.

Peter sees suffering as a kind of foretaste or reflection of the great day of judgement (vv17, 18). Believers will be spared at the judgement on account of their faith in Jesus, the human race's perfect representative. He has born the sentence of our unadmitted and unforgiven sin. The end which awaits unbelievers is beyond imagination. 'For it is time for judgment to begin with the family of God; and if it begins with us, what will the outcome be for those who do not obey the gospel of God?' Peter backs up his thinking on this matter with a quotation from Proverbs 11:31: 'If it is hard for the righteous to be saved, what will become of the ungodly and the sinner?'

Don't give up!

Peter urges those of us who suffer (or find the going difficult) not to despair or to give up on our Christian faith. It is indeed very hard to remain loyal to Jesus, especially if the alternative is physical abuse, a beating or perhaps even death. In the early church at the time of Peter's writing Christians were often required perhaps on a given day in the year to come individually and present themselves before the Roman authorities. They were requested to offer incense and to say 'Caesar is Lord'. Those who were believers knew that only 'Jesus is Lord' and most refused to make the declaration. Their punishment was a severe beating or more likely the death penalty. There were some Christians who renounced their faith or obtained false certificates to say that they had sacrificed incense to Caesar when they hadn't in fact done so, rather than face torture or be thrown to wild beasts in the local arena. Yet even without the threat of this kind of suffering, it's still all too possible to take the easy course and turn our backs on Jesus. Peter urges us to adopt a different option: 'So then, those who suffer according to God's will should commit themselves to their faithful Creator and continue to do good.'

An example of this came to mind as I was reflecting on this exhortation. Martin Luther King was a black American Baptist pastor working in Alabama, USA, in the 1960s. He 'dreamed a dream', as he put it in his famous address, of an America totally freed from racial prejudice and injustice. In 1968 he was assassinated in Memphis and it seemed like the dream had come to an abrupt end. His wife, Coretta, could so easily have turned aside, a bitter and disillusioned woman; but she didn't. Instead she took up the mantle of her husband's vision and she continued 'to do good'. Despite this terrible setback, the result of human wickedness and fear, she believed ultimately that God is our 'faithful Creator'.

I can think immediately of several people whom I know who have passed through severely trying circumstances and yet have had the faith to keep positive and 'to do good'. A young wife with several children discovered her husband had been unfaithful. She forgave him, they were reconciled and a secure Christian marriage and family life developed. A dedicated young Christian husband's wife died of cancer leaving him with young children. He continued steadfast in his faith coping with his work and his young family.

The reason why they and we are able to trust God in the time of hardship or suffering is quite simply because he knows what it is at first hand to suffer. He came in the person of Jesus into this world of suffering and pain. In Jesus he experienced the hurt and the anguish of human injustice and brutality to the full. We can therefore rely on him to be with us whatever may come our way.

Discussion questions

1 Do you sometimes find yourself asking why doesn't God do something? In what situations would you particularly want God to be intervening at this moment in time?

2 In what ways do you feel Jesus could help someone you know who is suffering?

Chapter 11

A PURPOSE IN SERVING OTHERS

Being a servant is not an altogether popular notion these days. It is true we still speak of our top government officers as 'public servants' but for the most part our image of 'service' and 'servants' is a negative one. Servants are weak, feeble, cringing and perhaps something after the style of Baldric of Black Adder fame.

This kind of thinking is further reinforced by the high profile accorded to power politics, line management and the doctrine that the fittest survive. The image makers are in the business of promoting the real go-getters, the strong guys and the macho men. The people they want us to look up to are the Sylvester Stallones and Frank Brunos of this world. They're tough. They're real people. They know how to stand up for themselves.

Being a servant

Jesus' concept of greatness was the complete reverse of all this. On one occasion the mother of James and John, two of his disciples, came and asked where her sons were likely to get to in the promotion stakes. Jesus replied, 'Whoever wants to become great among you must be your servant, and whoever wants to be first must be your slave' (Matthew 20:26).

Jesus' call to all his people, and particularly to those in leadership, is to serve others.

To the elders among you, I appeal as a fellow-elder, a witness of Christ's sufferings and one who also will share in the glory to be revealed: Be shepherds of God's flock that is under your care, serving as overseers – not because you must, but because you are willing, as God wants you to be; not greedy for money, but eager to serve; not lording it over those entrusted to you, but being examples to the flock. And when the Chief Shepherd appears, you will receive the crown of glory that will never fade away.

Young men, in the same way be submissive to those who are older. All of you, clothe yourselves with humility towards one another, because,

'God opposes the proud but gives grace to the humble.'

Humble yourselves, therefore, under God's mighty hand, that he may lift you up in due time. Cast all your anxiety on him because he cares for you.

Be self-controlled and alert. Your enemy the devil prowls around like a roaring lion looking for someone to devour. Resist him, standing firm in the faith, because you know that your brothers throughout the world are undergoing the same kind of sufferings.

And the God of all grace, who called you to his eternal glory in Christ, after you have suffered a little while, will himself restore you and make you strong, firm and steadfast. To him be the power for ever and ever. Amen.

1 Peter 5:1–11

My wife attended a girls' school in North Wales. It's motto was *Non Ministrare Sed Ministrare* which means 'Not to be served but to serve'. This is exactly what Peter is prescribing in this last part of his letter. He wants Christians to be servant people. What he writes is specifically addressed to church leaders (elders) but we noted earlier that Peter regards all Christians as a priesthood (1 Peter 2:5) so what he says is applicable to all of us!

The Greek word for elder is *presbuteros* from which we derive the word 'presbyter' or 'presbyterian'. In the early Christian church of the New Testament, 'bishops', 'overseers', 'pastors' or 'shepherds' were all simply other terms for those whom Peter refers to here as 'elders'. This is born out in verse 2 when he tells the elders to 'be shepherds of God's flock' and to take care of or 'oversee' them. The Greek word for 'oversee' is the same as for 'bishop'.

So what does a clergyman do all day? Some people think not very much! The reality of the situation is that these days most clergy work far too hard. The question we should ask, however, is not what does the church leader do, but what *should* he do? Visit the neighbourhood or parish from door to door? Join the Samaritans and help the needy? Be involved in the local community, chairing welfare and schools committees? Try to reach the youth and build for a brighter church tomorrow? Throw all energy into evangelism and try to get as many people into the church as possible?

What should the elder do? Peter is in no doubt. The elder's concern is primarily for his 'flock'. The shepherd must guide and lead his sheep. The shepherd must protect and nourish them. The injured and the sickly must be lovingly tended and brought back to full health.

In other places in the New Testament further instructions are given to church elders, but still with the aim and purpose that they should care for their flock (1 Timothy 3:1–7; Titus 1:5–9; James 5:14, 15). So church leaders (or elders) are to be concerned with the people of God, with nourishing, protecting and encouraging them. As Peter wrote these words perhaps he was thinking of the incident in his own life which followed his denial of Jesus. After his resurrection Jesus asked Peter three times, 'Do you love me?' Each time Peter replied, 'Yes Lord, you know that I love you.' Each time Jesus replied, 'Take care of my sheep' (John 21:15–17).

One of the reasons why churches are sometimes weak is because clergy, instead of spending their time 'taking care of their sheep', pass their time doing other things. Peter reminds them here of their responsibility, that it is God's church, not theirs. If one of their flock is lost, a leader has lost someone else's property.

This first paragraph of chapter 5 is a particular reminder and a challenge to all who are in any kind of Christian leadership. Is sufficient effort made to teach those who have recently become Christians to pray and read the Bible? Do we really take the trouble to find out what's happening in the lives of those who are absent from our church or house group? Are there practical ways in which we can be helping Christians who are unwell or the families of those who are in hospital? Within all our fellowships there are relationships and families where there is stress and breakdown. Could we be offering to listen, help and pray at least in some of these situations? There are difficulties at school, college and work places. Do we as Christian leaders make the effort to find out how children and young people are faring in these situations? It is all too easy, especially if we're pressurised ourselves, to put such people to the back of our minds and hope that they are all right or that someone else will do something for them. How committed are we to caring for those who are part of the flock of God of which we are a part?

How to serve others

This part of the letter is, as we have seen, directed in the first instance to church leaders ('elders'). However, Peter goes on to address the younger members of the church (v5a), and finally everyone (v5b – 'one another'). He gives fairly detailed and practical advice as to how they should serve each other.

With willingness

Peter urges that elders should serve 'not because [they] must, but because [they] are willing'. People take on service in the church for all sorts of reasons. I heard someone say on one occasion, 'Remember, your only qualification for doing some of the jobs you do is your inability to say "No"!' It's all too easy to take on tasks out of a sense of guilt or pressure because we feel someone's got to do it. Perhaps it's good to remind ourselves that a need does not necessarily constitute a call. As a general principle it would seem that if God is calling us to a particular avenue of service he will put in us a glad and willing spirit to do it. Paul put it like this in his letter to the Philippians: 'it is God who works in you to will and to act according to his good purpose' (Philippians 2:13).

This is not to say that there won't be times of stress and difficulty in Christian service. Clearly there will. At such occasions we may well find ourselves wanting to give up or withdraw for a period. When these moments come, we need to hang in there at our task and be reluctant to succumb to an unwilling and disheartened spirit.

St Benedict was born in Rome at the close of the fifth century. He later founded the greatest monastic order of the Western Church. The Benedictines followed his rule which was based on obedience. True obedience, according to Benedict, is 'obedience of the heart'; it is 'obedience without delay'. If the abbot calls one of the brethren to a new service, whatever is being done must be left immediately. True obedience is constant and without fear or dawdling. All our service is to be done from a willing heart and spirit. People and churches are not likely to be blessed if they are led by leaders who grudge their time or wish they could be doing something else.

Not for wealth

At this point, Peter touches on the area of payment and money as it relates to Christian service. He's not objecting to the idea of a paid ministry, nor is he against pastors and church workers receiving a living wage. In fact it seems to have been the case that most of the early Christian leaders received pitifully low pay. This was because many of the churches were small and the members weren't from the wealthy sectors of society. The same is true of most church leaders today, particularly in the UK. Churches need to adopt a much more generous attitude to those who serve them. Despite this, it does seem from Peter's warning and others elsewhere in the New Testament (1

Timothy 3:3,8) that there were those who wanted more money.

The question of financial payments for Christian service is not something which will effect most of us since the majority of churches in this country have very few paid members of staff. Nevertheless, Peter reminds those who do receive money for Christian work to be careful that they don't set their hearts on it. The history of the Christian church, both in the distant past and the recent present, is littered with individuals who have been corrupted by money and wealth. Many of the great monastic houses had begun originally with vows of poverty, but lost their way spiritually because they became rich through the land they came to own and their trading commodities such as wool. More recently the world has witnessed money corrupting the televangelism of Jim Bakker who went to prison in 1989 for taking and misusing billions of dollars given by his followers to his 'Praise the Lord' ministries.

Not for self-satisfaction

Here is a general point which is applicable to all of us. We must scrupulously avoid doing any form of Christian service for what we can get out of it. Our motive must always be to give, never to get. It's all too easy for a church leader to build up a congregation round his or her own personality, to satisfy his or her own need instead of doing it for the Lord whose church it is, and out of love for him. The same could apply just as much in the case of a house group or a Sunday school. Which of us is entirely free of this kind of self-seeking?

Not for power

Peter tells Christian leaders that they must not be 'lording it over' those entrusted to them. Church officers are not to behave like petty tyrants; they are to be servants. This was the pattern and example which Jesus himself laid down for us. He warned his disciples against being like the gentile rulers 'who lord it over' others. Instead, he said that whoever wants to be great must become the servant of all (Matthew 20:24–28).

Our human nature is such that for many people prestige and influence over others is often more gripping even than money. In recent decades we have seen some sad and disastrous consequences which have resulted from Christian leaders taking it upon themselves to dictate and control the lives of others. A teaching emanated from America in the late 1960s which required members to submit to and obey their church leaders in every aspect of their living. I myself have encountered instances of people being told who to marry, or forbidden to move house and job. This kind of dominance by leaders was in part an attempt to counteract the lack of pastoral care in the main-line denominational churches and also a reaction to the moral laxity of the period coupled with declining parental and school discipline. In more recent years many churches with such 'shepherding' policies have come to more balanced views on the matter.

Clearly it's good that people should have the opportunity to seek advice and guidance from church leaders and to have them pray for wisdom and direction. In the end, however, each individual person needs to be left free to choose their own course of action before God. It is only as people are left to make their own decisions, even if these are not always the wisest, that they will have at least the possibility of maturing as Christians and as people. Where people allow someone else, even another Christian, to run their life for them, there is always the danger of producing a 'Waco style' cult. Such misguided communities and the resulting emotionally damaged people could be avoided if Christian leaders take note of Peter's guidance.

Submit to each other

In verse 5 Peter is speaking particularly to the younger members of the churches he was writing to (the word he used means simply 'younger'). It's possible that some of them were becoming dissatisfied with their leadership and feeling that elders were not reacting strongly enough to the crisis which surrounded them in the hostile Roman Empire. They are urged 'to be submissive to those who are older' and 'to clothe themselves with humility towards one another'. We need humility in two directions: we should be humble towards each other and humble towards God. 'Humble yourselves, therefore, under God's mighty hand . . .'

It's often said that you can tell a nation by the way in which it treats its older generation. Peter urges younger Christians in particular to be submissive to those who are older. In this he was in line with the Old Testament teaching on holiness (see Leviticus 19:32). It's often the older people within our fellowships who know what we really need to hear, if only we have the good grace and humility to listen.

To be humble to one another means that we should be prepared to serve each other, particularly in the little things. I was quite struck by an incident which happened in a local school in my home town. A teacher was on his hands and knees collecting the remains of a glass bottle which someone had smashed. An eighteen year old school prefect came along and said, 'Oh Sir, you shouldn't be doing that. Shall I go and get a first year?'! To be humble towards each other means to be willing to do menial, practical jobs for each other. Humility is an attitude of mind as well as action. It means coming to the other person, whoever they are, in an attitude of wanting to help and care for them in whatever way is necessary.

We also need humility in the way in which we listen and speak to one another. We all find this a difficult one, but are we willing to work on it? If we feel we have been listened to, our relationship with the other person is deepened. The fellowship or Christian group to which we belong is also strengthened.

A further aspect of humility is our willingness to make an apology. When did we last say sorry or admit we were wrong to someone in our congregation or to our partner? It's not always easy to say, 'I am so sorry I spoke foolishly' or 'My behaviour was out of order'. We need to clothe ourselves with humility towards one another.

We also need to be humble towards God. There is a certain kind of person who says to himself, 'I don't need help with this. I am strong, educated and articulate. I can cope.' If this is our mind-set, we should take care because, as has often been said, 'Pride comes before a fall'. If we go it alone and try to cope with everything by our own endeavours what we are in effect saying is, 'I don't need God's help. I can manage.' Be humble enough to look to the Lord for strength. Part of humility is being willing to let God and others do things for us, to pray for us and to give to us.

After the last supper, Jesus took a towel and started to wash his disciples' feet. When he got to Peter, Peter said, 'No, Lord, you shall never wash my feet.' He was too proud to let someone do something menial for him. He was Peter the rock, the macho fisherman, the leader. 'Yes, Lord,' he was in effect saying, 'though all these others deny you, I am Peter and I will never deny you.'

The towel which Jesus took at the last supper was a special shape. It had two ends which were tied or 'clothed' around the waist. In the Greek language there's a special word for this. When Peter writes here 'Clothe yourselves with humility', he's using the very same word that is used of Jesus on that day when he clothed himself with the towel and washed his disciples' feet.

Humility means we're always ready to learn, receive and be served by others. Peter didn't learn humility in a day and neither will we. Nevertheless he's urging us to be willing. Are we?

Without anxiety

In verse 7 Peter says, 'Cast all your anxiety on him because he cares for you.' This is said in the context of Christian leadership and service. Peter was the one whom Jesus had appointed leader of his church. At the time when he wrote this letter he had responsibility for numerous churches scattered across the Mediterranean area. Like Paul he knew the daily pressure of being concerned for all the churches (see 2 Corinthians 11:28).

Christian work, and church leadership in particular, can be both stressful and demanding in terms of the time and energy which it requires. Dealing with people's problems and coping with their different agendas is a heavy commitment. It is small wonder that ministers' marriages sometimes break down, elders' children go off the rails or factions split our fellowships. Clergy burn-out is a growing phenomenon it seems.

Peter has already underlined for us the fact that the church is God's church. Ultimately, it's his responsibility. The people are his and their salvation is his work. It is God who must meet people in their needs if anything of lasting value is to take place in their lives. Therefore in the last analysis we can rest all anxieties we may have about the church and church matters with God. But how can we do this? I suggest we must deliberately and consciously get ourselves into the Lord's presence and say to him out loud: 'Lord, I am giving you the burden of our church's financial affairs, the pain of that person's disloyalty, the stress over the style of worship, the differences of opinion over how the house groups are to be organised, the divisive influence of . . .'

Somewhere among our books at home we have a paperback called *Brethren Hang Loose*. It tells the story of an American minister who was called to a fashionable city church which was just beginning a downward spiral in terms of membership, finances and status. He had been brought in to stem the tide and tried everything he could think of. There were new evangelism ideas, a revamping of the music and stewardship campaigns, but still the slide downward continued. Eventually the minister had a total breakdown. The church were kind and paid for him and his wife to have a summer holiday. One day while he was lying on the beach he found himself hitting the sand with clenched fists. He cried out, 'Lord, I've tried everything I can think of.' As he lay there in the stillness with the noise of the sea in the background he heard quite distinctly a voice saying, 'Now let me have a go!' He returned home to hang loose and let the Lord bear the weight of responsibility for what was after all his church. Needless to say, the situation was transformed.

Be self-controlled

Whoever said Christianity is easy stuff! Being self-controlled is not the name of the game in the present generation. All the ads, all the media, everything tells us the reverse. Indulge yourself. A little of what you fancy will do you no harm. A lot of what you fancy could be wonderfully liberating! The bottom line is we either control ourselves (self-control) or something else controls us. The problem, as Peter sees it, is that if we allow something to dominate our lives totally, the devil can use that thing to get a grip on us. It might be food, drink, money, sex, work, houses, land, books, videos, drugs, church work, gossiping, slander, counselling others, clothes, temper, shopping, politics or whatever. Anything which starts to control us can put us under the devil's influence. Church leaders and Christian workers are not immune from these things. In fact they are often more easily caught by them because when under stress the temptation is to take comfort in them. Be warned, says Peter, 'the devil prowls around like a roaring lion looking for someone to devour' (v8).

What's the answer if we feel we're losing control in some area of our lives? We must stand 'firm in the faith' (v9) in fellowship with other Christians ('your brothers') and '*resist* him'. How do we resist the devil? By adopting an active and positive mind-set. Jesus cried out on one occasion, 'Get behind me Satan.' If

147

Jesus found it necessary to do such a thing, we're surely going to have to do the same. So if we're sitting in our office or home and we catch ourselves thinking some revengeful or lustful thought, or plotting some spiteful course of action, we must quite simply call out, 'Jesus, I reject that thought' or 'Help me, Jesus' or 'Satan, get out!'

One of Jesus' least popular teachings was his so called 'strong teaching'. 'If your right eye causes you to sin, gouge it out and throw it away.' 'If your right hand causes you to sin, cut it off and throw it away' (Matthew 5:29,30). He didn't of course intend that we should do this literally. What he meant was this: if looking at a particular person causes you to lust, don't keep looking at them. If the clothes-shop window causes you to overspend, walk somewhere else. If a particular activity is damaging you, keep your hands away from it.

To sum up this point, when the going gets tough and stressful in our Christian service, and we are tempted to give up or seek comfort elsewhere, we must take refuge in God. The secret of resistance is to stand firm in our faith and actively to resist the devil.

The results of serving others

Finally in verses 10 and 11 Peter reminds us of some of the benefits which will result if we serve one another with these qualities in our lives. God, he says, will restore us and make us 'strong, firm and stead-fast'. The word Peter uses for 'restore' is sometimes used of repairing or refitting a damaged vessel. In Mark 1:19 it's used for mending fishing nets. Something of this idea may be in Peter's thoughts. After the hurt and pain of persecution or maybe the stress of Christian service, God will repair the damaged areas so that we can continue to serve him effectively. God will also make us strong. We all have moments of weakness where we perhaps have lost control or compromised or wavered in our faith. God will give us that capacity to be firm and solid about the things that really matter. This is a truly vital quality to have in any kind of church leadership role.

Peter also mentions the quality of 'firmness'. In the middle of the toughest times of church leadership God will give to us the capacity to be 'firm'. Just as an athlete emerges from the rigour of his training with a new toughness of muscle and fibre, so the Lord will toughen those who serve him faithfully. Finally he will make us able to 'stand fast'. God will make his servants aware that they are standing on rock solid ground. Nothing will cave in under them. On Christ, the solid rock, they stand. All other ground is sinking sand.

Discussion questions

1 Do you think that the Christian call to be servants is unrealistic in the pressurised world of today?
2 A prayer in the Church of England Prayer Book speaks of our serving Christ as being perfect freedom. In what ways do you find this to be true?

Chapter 12

A PURPOSE IN LIVING

With the help of Silas, whom I regard as a
faithful brother, I have written to you briefly,
encouraging you and testifying that this is the
true grace of God. Stand fast in it.
She who is in Babylon, chosen together with
you, sends you her greetings, and so does my
son Mark. Greet one another with a kiss of love.
Peace to all of you who are in Christ.

1 Peter 5:12–14

It's a common practice when we write a letter to slip
in the most important thing right at the end. So just
before we sign off 'with love' or 'yours sincerely' we
say it: 'Please make sure you're there in plenty of
time'; 'Please don't resign'; 'Please help us with this
project'. This is what Peter does. Right at the end of
his letter, he says something of real importance. If you
have begun to have this purpose in your life, stay
with it! 'Stand fast in it' (v12).

The word which is translated 'stand fast' was used
in the Greek language for standing your ground in a
wrestling match. In the bouts which took place in the
Roman games, the moment you were pushed down
to the ground or out of your territory the contest was
lost. The all important thing therefore was to hold

your ground. The background to Peter's words here is very similar to that of Ephesians 6:10–18. There Paul also has a picture of a wrestling match in the back of his mind as he talks about the fight and the struggle which Christians have in their daily lives. We're up against evil spiritual forces, but we must stand our ground. Three times Paul urges us to arm ourselves spiritually and stand (v13).

There are many people who have begun to live their lives with the purpose which only Jesus can give, but then they have given up. The going has got too tough. They have become weary or frustrated. Difficulties along the way have discouraged them.

If we stop and think about it for a moment, anything which is rewarding or worthwhile will inevitably be strenuous. I was reading an article written just recently about a famous actress. She related something of the hard graft which is involved in acting. She described how she came home late at night after having played in an evening performance. But even before bed, she needed to take a glass of wine and spend time learning her lines for the next part. If she didn't live with this kind of steady discipline, next time there would be no place for her in the world of film or theatre.

Jesus never promised that finding our purpose in living for him would be easy. He taught that in the world we would have troubles (John 16:33) and to follow him would be like carrying a cross (Mark 8:34). Christians are part of the same world as everybody else and we're going to have to grapple with the very same issues. In a Christian home, for example, we will find the same differences of opinion, the same issues with the children, the same sorts of sexual difficulties, financial hassles and bereavements as in any other.

The one big difference, however, will be that we have the added perspective, help and strength which Jesus alone can give us. Olympic medallist Kriss Akabusi put it like this: 'I don't really know what the future holds but I'm perfectly content to know it's in God's hands.'

In his closing greeting Peter mentions two fellow Christians who had lived with this purpose without flinching or giving up. There is Silas (or Silvanus) whom he describes 'as a faithful brother' who has helped him in the writing of this letter. He also mentions Mark whom he describes as his son.

• *Silas* was present at the Council of Jerusalem (see Acts 15) where he is described as a leader among the brothers. He was charged with the special responsibility of making the Council's decisions known to a number of churches in Asia Minor. For a long time he travelled with Paul as his right-hand man. Together they journeyed to Philippi where they taught the Christian message and expelled a spirit of fortune telling from a slave girl. As a result they were both attacked by an angry mob and the magistrates had them whipped and beaten. Silas also preached with Paul at Corinth (2 Corinthians 1:19). He was a Roman citizen (Acts 16:38) and for that reason would have been much better educated than Peter. Silas was someone who found a real purpose in taking second place, first behind Paul and now here behind Peter.

• *Mark*, whom Peter mentions in verse 13, may be the same Mark who worked with Barnabas in Cyprus (see Acts 15:37) and later with Paul (2 Timothy 4:11). He is probably the Mark who, tradition says, wrote Peter's gospel. Papias, a church leader who lived in the early second century and who was taught by the apostle John, collected and wrote down a number of early Christian traditions. In one of them he relates how Mark wrote down the teachings of Peter.

> Mark, who was Peter's interpreter, wrote down accurately, though not in order all that he recollected of what Christ had said and done. For he was not a hearer of the Lord or a follower of His; he followed Peter as I have said, at a later date, and Peter adapted his instructions to practical needs without any attempt to give the Lord's words systematically.

Here were two leaders in the early Christian Church who had faithfully worked alongside Peter. They had found purpose in living their lives for Jesus. It is important to underline the fact that full-time work for the church is not a superior sphere in which greater purpose and satisfaction can automatically be found. The important thing is for each of us to find the course of life for which we are most fitted and then to do that to the best of our ability. As Paul put it in another place in the New Testament: 'Whatever you do, work at it with all your heart, as working for the Lord, not for men' (Colossians 3:23).

Peter's letter is a word for us today. He is insisting that the most worthwhile goal or purpose we can have is to know the presence of Jesus within us and to live our lives serving him. There are countless millions of people throughout the ages who have come to this realisation. Svetlana Stalin, the daughter of the Russian dictator, Joseph Stalin, grew up in a communist household where there was never any conversation about God. Later as an adult she was able to make sense of her life as a result of making a Christian commitment. She said:

> When I became a grown up person, I found that it was impossible to exist without God in one's heart.

Gavin Peacock, the Chelsea footballer said:

> Having my faith gives me a perspective on life and I know that although football is my job, it's not the be all and end all.

Malcolm Muggeridge, journalist, broadcaster and editor of *Punch* magazine, had a long and searching journey through life. Eventually he was able to rediscover Jesus in a personal way. He said in 1968:

> I am more convinced than I am in my own existence that the view of life Christ came into the world to preach, and died to sanctify, remains as true and as valid as ever, and that all who care to, young and old, healthy and infirm, wise and foolish, may live thereby, finding in our troubled, confused world, as in all other circumstances and at all other times, an enlightenment and a serenity not otherwise attainable.

My hope is that we are able to live our lives in the spirit of Malcolm Muggeridge's words. If we can, we will know what it is to be living with a purpose!

Discussion questions

1 Gavin Peacock said that his faith in Christ has given him a 'perspective on life'. In what ways has your faith in Christ affected your perspective on life?

2 At the end of his letter Peter urges us to 'stand fast' as Christians. How can we do this and become stronger and more active in our Christian commitment?

3 How can we help others to find a purpose in living?